Mastering Money

A Simple Guide to Achieving Financial Success

Inga Chira, Ph.D., CFP®

For Mike:

Thank you for encouraging me when I need it.
Thank you for telling me I can do it.
And thank you for being there for me.

For Christopher:

Thank you for being the best little boy out there.

Contents

Introduction

Welcome to the party

It's your money. The more you know about managing it, the more you get to keep.

If you are reading a personal finance book, chances are it's either because you are excited to learn more about the topic or because someone is making you. I teach personal finance courses, and every semester, I have the same goal: to get my students from the latter (reluctant) to the former (excited).

Many start reading and learning about personal finance because it's a requirement of passing the course. But by the end, my students often say that this is knowledge everyone needs. I totally agree. I am passionate about the subject and think everyone should be required to take it in college.

My logic is very simple: I don't care what major you are/were/will be in college or what you do in life. We all must pay bills, buy cars and homes, pay taxes, and worry about money. Despite my great liberal arts education, I am sure a personal finance course would have served me just a bit better than the African drumming class that fulfilled my mandatory art class requirement. Don't get me wrong—I loved playing the djembe in a circle with all the fraternity boys. But I am convinced that knowing the basics of personal finance is an imperative skill for having a better life.

Now, I am not delusional. I do not expect that, after reading this book, you will replace me as a CFP® or spend your free time listening to finance podcasts. But I hope that, at the very least, I will sell you on the importance of this topic and that you will care enough to do the best you can with your own life and money.

Financial preparedness typically leads to a life full of abundance and success. It also reduces stress and gives us a feeling of control over our lives. I see many of my students dreaming and aiming big. This is one of my favorite traits in those who have their whole lives ahead of them. By combining the desire to succeed with financial preparedness, you can build and live the life that you want.

There are many roadblocks on the path to financial well-being. You might end up in a relationship that has a negative impact on your money situation. You might encounter health issues, career change plans, failed businesses, peer pressure or even deceit related to money or life in general.

When you know what's important to you, however, it is less likely you'll fall into these traps. Stacking your financial future in your favor when you are young increases the probability you will succeed later on.

Before we start, here is a little background on me. I knew in middle school that I would eventually study business, but it wasn't until my freshman year in college that I decided to study finance. Okay, the true story: I declared international business to be my major, but quickly realized it wouldn't get me specific skills. The more specific skills you have, the more employable you become, so I added finance as a second major. Then, just because two majors are never enough, I decided to also add marketing.

In case you are wondering, no one needs three majors, and if I were to do it all over again, I would major in finance and pick random classes to get exposure to things I would otherwise know nothing about. In other words, I would have taken advantage of that liberal arts education when I had the chance. That's just a side note in case you are still in college and need some career advice. Let's get back to finance.

I majored in finance. I graduated from college with a 4.0 GPA and was the College of Business Student of the Year. I got a gold medal and had finance internships at two big companies by the time I graduated.

And guess what? I had no idea what my credit score was or that you should sign up for a credit card for reasons other than the free bag of M&Ms a credit card company offers you in the cafeteria. This, by the way, is how I got my first credit card as a freshman. Thank you, Discover, for helping me build a credit history when I didn't know I needed one.

There you go. You now know my first secret, and if this book goes the way I hope, you will learn plenty more. What I learned from that experience is that somehow, within the US educational system, it is possible to be the best finance major in the whole university and have no idea how to make a basic personal finance decision while being paid to make corporate finance decisions.

A few jobs in finance later, I now have an MBA, about 10 years of experience teaching finance, a Ph.D. in finance, a CFP®, and my own financial planning practice. I think I finally know something about personal finance. If you know me well, you also know that I will talk about these topics to anyone who will listen to me because they change your life.

Most people assume I was born telling others what to do with their money. No, that's not true. I started getting a real interest in personal finance right after college, when I moved from the cocoon of campus, in a nice dorm with a meal plan, to the rough streets of Jacksonville, Florida.

It wasn't that rough, really. I was living in a gated community. About the same time, I met my future husband. Despite his profession—pilot—he was a wizard when it came to understanding his credit score, financial responsibility and having his money stuff together. That's right, my crush, future boyfriend, future husband, future baby daddy sat me down and gave me a great primer on credit scores and building credit. And I was like ... what? This is finance? I can do this for a living instead of writing boring Excel formulas all day long?

Thirteen years later, yep, I can attest that I am indeed doing this for a living and I love it. I only hope to pass along just a little bit of my enthusiasm to you.

Okay, now about this book. Who is this book for and what should you expect from it? Here are some bullet points for you. You will learn soon enough about my obsession with organization and bullet points, and there is no better time to start than in the introduction.

- This book is designed for college students and youngish people who might have skipped this part of their education so far but are now interested in learning how to get their money life together. In other words, this book is for anyone who wants to learn the basics of personal finance. (A special shout-out to the students in my personal finance courses who told me what college students want to hear about and what they couldn't care less about in a book on personal finance. I mostly listened to you because a professor doesn't always know everything. Thank you for your helpful suggestions.)

- If you are not a 22-year-old college student but need to learn about specific topics like investments, how to talk to your spouse about money or insurance, flip to the chapter that interests you. Each chapter was designed to be read as needed.

- I've presented the information just like I do with my students. If it sounds too "financy," it's no good. This is not rocket science, and everyone should be able to understand what I am saying. Finance people are so used to their jargon they might not have any idea that the way they talk intimidates others. I hope not to do that, and I am sorry if I slip and use terms like "diversifying your portfolio" too often.

- Each chapter is structured in roughly the same way. There is plenty of research that shows we learn better by creating patterns and repetition.

We start with a story or a few examples in the beginning. All the stories are real. They are mine or a client's, and yes, I've changed all the names except mine. I then move into explaining the concept, giving you my perspective on the topic and the answers to the questions I get all the time, identified throughout the book as "My $.02." Finally, I conclude with a few main action-item points for you to take away and think about or do, along with some space for you to grab a pen and plot your mission.

I would like to emphasize that we all think our situation is somehow different, somehow special, but it is important to understand that money has patterns. The problems we encounter are universal. Yes, there are exceptions, but this book is not written for the trust fund kid. (If you are a trust fund kid, you can still read this book and then give me all your money to manage.)

Most of us go to college to make a better life for ourselves. We have bills; we may have student loans. We start our careers with little money and then, as we get more money, we get more responsibilities and even more bills. Houses, kids, master's degrees, vacations, worrying about retirement—trust me, that day will come. It all piles up. As my friend Nick says, we all go through the same cycle. And I want this book to be a guide to the important things most of us will encounter in life. I want this book to help you.

My main goal is to be as easy to understand and specific as possible. I will also give you my opinions about things and tell you what I did or would do instead of giving you another definition or finance term.

Many finance books avoid opinions. I will say this many times as well: it depends. But where possible, I would like to explain where I am coming from and why I would make one decision over another. I'm not offering solutions for everyone, but in the end, are you not paying for an opinion when you go to a finance professional? This book represents my opinions. Please refer to the disclosure section for more details. There is also a lot of personal stuff in here. With that in mind, we are almost ready to start. There is just one more question to answer.

"Who are you, lady, anyways?"

Officially, we can say that I have a Ph.D. in finance and I am a Certified Financial Planner. For a living, I tell people how to spend their hard-earned money. That must count for something, right? I am currently an Assistant Professor of Finance and Financial Planning, and I have my own virtual registered investment advisory firm.

Here is the English translation: I teach personal finance, financial planning, and corporate finance to undergraduate and MBA students. I also work with people to help them manage their paychecks without running out of money, help them invest, and help them make better money-related decisions. I am pretty sure some of them also use me as a secondary therapist.

In addition, I do research in the field of financial planning. I look at why some people save for retirement and others do not; why being educated, even very educated, does not necessarily mean that you are good with your money; how financial planners can help regular folks—you know, topics that all of us ponder on all day long.

Unofficially, I like finance. *Like* is probably an understatement, given that I think relaxing in the morning by sipping coffee and reading the *InvestmentNews* or power-walking and listening to finance podcasts is as enjoyable as it gets. I get excited when the newest issue of the *Journal of Financial Planning* shows up in the mail, and I love a good finance story more than I like a funny cat video on Facebook, although I like those too.

My $.02

What is the most important financial lesson you can teach me?

Before we go to the first chapter and have to do some work, I would like to leave you with the one thing I get asked about a lot. After being in the finance industry for more than 15 years, what is the most important financial lesson I can share?

Be willing to talk about money. That's it. The more transparent and unashamed you are about your money situation, the better. There is nothing wrong with where you are right now. There is nothing wrong with not knowing anything about finance or about knowing plenty but still not trusting yourself 100% with making financial decisions.

That's what I want you to remember. No shame. Be open, seek help and ask questions because, at the end of the day, it is your life and your money. What someone else thinks about it is irrelevant.

Sorry if you expected advice on how to become uber-mega-rich!

Your Bullet Point To-Do List

- Download the *Radical Personal Finance Podcast*. Listen to one episode that appeals to you each week. Start your money education and keep expanding your knowledge. Every Monday, write down which episode you listened to and what it was about.

- Write what you currently do not like about your money life. Is it your credit card debt? Is it the fact that you feel like you don't understand this topic? Anything goes. Write it down. Use bullet points. Send them to me if you want approval. You can find me on Facebook on my personal page (Inga Chira) or on my business page (Attainable Wealth). You can also find me on LinkedIn (Inga Chira). Expect lots of baby pictures though. It used to be cat pictures, but now I have a baby so he wins.
https://www.facebook.com/inga.chira
https://www.facebook.com/AttainableWealth/
www.linkedin.com/in/inga-chira

- Write down what you consider the biggest financial mistake you have made so far. Now, write down your biggest financial win and your wisest financial decision so far. It does not have to be impressive. Done? Great. Cross out the mistake. There is no such thing. Write down what you learned from it. There is always something to learn, so really, it's a win. You are ready to start, and I am excited to follow along with you.

- Get yourself a financial journal and write everything useful you learn about money in it. Sit down, open your journal. Get one for $.69 from the grocery store if you don't have one. There is no need to spend $20 on a fancy journal unless that's the only way you will care about finance. Then it's okay to say goodbye to the $20. Keep this journal, write in it and come back to it periodically to reread what you wrote.

PART I:
GETTING YOUR
MONEY STUFF
TOGETHER

Chapter 1

Mastering your cash

Making budgets glamorous again

To illustrate the importance of a budget, or cash flow plan or wealth map—whatever you'd prefer to call it—let me introduce you to two of my clients.

Jenny is a high school teacher in Los Angeles who makes around $80,000 per year. Although this would be a great income in many places, it is not that much in LA. What is more amazing is that she is maximizing her retirement account every year and is living on about $60,000. She can also pay her mortgage, go skiing, and invest, among many other things. She feels like she has a very successful life. And get this: although she still has about 10 years to retirement, she has over a million dollars in her investment accounts. She hired me mostly to make sure she is not missing anything and that everything is set when she is ready to retire.

Jim makes about $300,000 per year, has two children in public high school and is struggling to pay his bills. He saves only a small percentage of his income in his retirement account. He has four car payments, a huge mortgage and lots of credit card debt. Jim hired me to help him figure out how to get out of debt. Despite being in his late 40s, he has almost no savings for emergencies or retirement. If he lost his job today, he would not be able to pay his bills in two months.

How is it possible that two people with vastly different incomes are in such different financial situations? Does making $80k in your 50s sound like a lot to you? How about $300k in your 40s? No matter what you believe a good income is, we can all agree that $300k should be enough to pay your bills, even in Los Angeles.

What is the problem? Why such a big difference?

The answer is in the lifestyle each of these two people chose to adopt. While one is driving a five-year-old Honda, the other is paying for four cars, two of which are for his high school children.

There is nothing wrong with either scenario if you can afford it, but it was obvious from the first time we met that Jim is stressed out about money. He does not want to be in the situation he is in.

So how do we change this?

At the core of financial success is one concept: more money must come in than goes out.

That's it. If you always remember this idea and put it into practice, your life will be easy. I call this the "Money-In, Money-Out" concept just because I hate the term *budgeting*. Budgeting creates the feeling of constraint, of not being able to live the life you want to live and do the things you want to do. It does not have to be like that.

Your mental attitude towards spending is way more important than the amount of money you make. You can do almost anything you want, as long as you plan for it.

As much as we all want to be rich and fabulous (maybe you don't, but many people do), it is essential to stop and remove yourself from your current lifestyle to ask a few questions.

Here is what I want you to think about:

- Are you happy with your financial situation today?

- Is there anything that stresses you out— anything you would like to remove from your life—money-wise?

- What kind of lifestyle do you want? What is important to you? Are you the person who is comfortable driving an old Honda, or is a nicer car important to you? Do you want to live in a big house, or do you prefer a smaller place and lots of travel/shoes/something else?

There is no wrong answer. Come up with whatever you think will make you happy. But think about these things. They will determine how you build your own cash flow map and what you save for, indulge in, and decide that you want to cut from your life.

Remember that the way to consistently get ahead in life financially is to spend less than you make. Period. It does not matter how much money you earn if, like Jim, you spend more than you make. There is no other way. I know, I know; you could win the lottery or marry rich. But the odds are awfully slim to bet your happiness on. Let's remove those disempowering ideas from the equation and focus on the things you can control.

Ask yourself frankly and without judgment: do you know where your money goes every month? And if you don't, why not? Is it because you are afraid to find out? Is it because you think you don't have the skills? The good thing is that we can solve that problem. If you can figure out how to use Snapchat filters, you can figure out where your money is going. Or is it because you never even thought to consider the question?

That all stops now, today. You will figure out where your money is going.

I am a big sucker for a good Excel spreadsheet. Mine is very simple. On the top, I have all the monthly income. On the bottom, I list all expenses; not the imaginary, "I wish these were my expenses," but the reality of what is going on in my life. If you get paid weekly or biweekly, you can do yours to match your paychecks.

The spreadsheet is a promise to yourself about how you will spend your money—before you get paid and start spending it. See the next page for what my spreadsheet looks like.

You want that last line, INCOME-EXPENSES, to be positive. In other words, you want your total income to be bigger than your total expenses. Otherwise, we have a problem, and no matter how much you try to make your situation better, it won't happen.

Many people tell me they don't even know where to start; how do they figure out their expenses? If you use debit and credit cards most of the time, then life is simple these days. All you need to do is sign up for an app that does it for you. There are a gazillion of them. The ones I like are Mint, Personal Capital and YNAB (You Need a Budget). The first two are free (well, you get bombarded with commercials, but that's a small price to pay).

YNAB is about $5 per month. Students can get a free version here:
https://www.youneedabudget.com/landing/college/.

Take a look. I personally love YNAB, but I've used all three and they are all good.

Here is how all these apps work. You link your debit and credit cards, and all your transactions automatically appear. You log in and set up a budget, whatever you think you will spend and want to spend in a month. Then, once a day or once a week, you go in and categorize the transactions. For example, a 7-Eleven transaction may be filed under gas, but it was really coffee you bought, so you change it from gas to food/coffee or whatever category you set up.

Table 1: The Money-In, Money-Out Fun

INCOME CATEGORIES		INCOME
1	Salary 1	
2	Salary 2	
3	Pension 1	
4	Other income?	
	TOTAL INCOME	$0.00

EXPENSE CATEGORIES		EXPENSES
1	Mortgage or Rent	
2	Light	
3	Water	
4	Cable	
5	Gas	
6	Phone	
7	Groceries	
8	Eating out	
9	Medical bills	
10	Insurance (add different lines for car, life, etc)	
11	Client 1 fun money - do whatever you want with this	
12	Client 2 fun money - do whatever you want with this	
13	Children expenses	
14	Travel	
15	Entertainment	
16	Car expenses	
17	Retiremement savings	
18	Gym	
19	Anything else? Keep adding lines until you are done	
	TOTAL EXPENSES	$0.00
	INCOME - EXPENSES	$0.00

These systems are smart. They will tell you how close you are to your desired limit or how much you went over budget. And then you will adjust your budget for next month. Fine-tune your budget every month until you get to a point where what you thought you would spend is what you actually spent.

If you use cash, you will need to keep track of your expenses and enter them into the system manually.

The best cash flow systems I have seen combine an Excel spreadsheet with an app that keeps track of your expenses. You write down your promises in Excel and set up those categories in your app. Once the month is over, you transfer the totals from the app back to Excel. You put them side by side with your promises and see how you did. Did you stick to your promises, or do you need to make some adjustment for the next month?

It is important to realize that you can't change your habits overnight. It normally takes three to 12 months to get good at this, to become aware of your spending and put changes into place. As long as you keep working at it, your habits and your life will change.

Doing nothing and wondering why your credit card bill is increasing every month won't do much for you. Trust me. Sitting down to figure out where your money is going so you can stop the bleeding and save for things that are important to you will work. So pick one of these apps or Google some others and let's get to setting up the unglamorous budget.

Back to our friends Jenny and Jim. How is it possible that Jenny has over a million dollars in investments? No, she did not invest in the next Apple stock. What she did was make a conscious choice to treat savings as a bill. After the "don't spend more than you make" concept, the next thing I hope I can convince you of is that **starting early and saving consistently will take you to a really good place in life.**

For this to happen, you need to treat savings as a bill and not as something that's left over after you went to Mexico for spring break, bought all your friends a round of drinks on a Saturday night or went to Vegas to try to make up that rent money you just spent in Mexico.

Savings is a bill, just like your electrical bill or your car payment. I will say it again. There should be a line on your budget that has a dollar amount, and that money does not exist for anything else.

How do you determine the dollar amount to save? If you have credit card debt, start small: $10 per paycheck is better than nothing. Promise yourself to increase it by $2 or $5 or whatever you can every month. Experiment. There is no wrong answer. I won't come after you to tell you the amount you are saving is not "correct" because what's right for you is too much or too little for someone else. So just do something already and start saving.

When I asked my students last semester what they would like to see in a personal finance book, they mentioned "something about sticking to your budget while being under tremendous peer pressure." I promise you more on this in Chapter 12, but for right now, if this applies to you, ask yourself why you feel uncomfortable and under pressure. Is it because you want to do things with your friends that require money and your friends don't understand your "budget problem"? Or is it maybe because you don't like to talk about money? Figure out what is bothering you so we can solve it later.

Lots of people I talk to say that budgeting makes them feel poor or that it requires too much work. I can't do much about the latter; yes, it requires two or three hours to set up your app and put together the categories.

I do, however, have a problem with the idea that building a budget will make you feel poor. If you do this right and put together a plan, you will not feel poor. You will feel empowered.

I've lost count of how many clients and students have told me that understanding where the money goes and how much they need to cut or save made them feel like they got it.

You will have control, and you will feel like you are on top of things. That's why we are doing this, people. You can't change your habits if you are not aware of them—so let's become aware of what's going on now.

My $.02

What is a reasonable budget? What categories should I have, and how much should I have in each of them?

Sorry to disappoint, but this is something only you can answer. Go back to what is important to you and the lifestyle you want. No one is judging you, and if they are, you don't want them as your friends anyway.

As I tell my clients, I don't care what you spend your money on as long as we agree about how much we spend on that something and stick to it. My sister spends lots of money on her dog. I spend lots of money on my nanny. My husband spends (or used to before he sold it) lots of money on his car. There is no right or wrong. Spend your money any way you want. Just tell me what you will do so I, or that app you chose, can hold you accountable.

Your Bullet Point To-Do List

- Choose an app to track your budget, and then set up your account. Spend an hour building your budget and linking all the credit and debit card accounts you use. If you find a great app I have not mentioned, let me know, as I am always on the lookout for a new and better one.

- Come back once a day for a whole month and compare your desired budget to the real one. How did you do? Are you close in each category? What would you like to cut, if anything? Is there any category you would like to increase because you know you will spend that money again?

- Repeat the process every paycheck for the next year. After a month or two, you can go from daily to weekly tracking. Adjust your budget until there are no more discrepancies.

Now, you got it. You are in control of your money.

Chapter 2

Getting the financial basics together

Moving out of your parents' basement

It's time to move out. Your parents deserve a break.

Whether you decided to get your own place when you turned 18 or you are currently 28, post-college, living with your parents again, almost every single one of us will need to get out at some point.

This chapter is for college students living at home or in student housing. If you are past that stage, but you have children or plan to someday, you might consider this information for their future.

This chapter focuses on the things to do before, during, and after moving out to survive on your own financially. A few people suggested that I include information on how to do laundry, but I think I will leave that to YouTube.

Amelia was one of my favorite students, and when I say favorite, I don't mean she got the best grades.

She barely got a B, but that was because she also worked two jobs, determined to take on as little debt as possible. She had the added pressure of immigrant parents who did not speak English and needed support. One day, she came to my office hours and said she worried about what would happen to her savings if her house burned down; she kept it all in cash in a box in her closet.

I had completely different conversations with Diane, another student in the same class. She got a car for her 16th birthday, her tuition was paid by her parents, and she had their credit card to use when needed. Yet, at 21, she was extremely responsible and looking for ways to prepare for life on her own.

As these two examples show you, our situations can be very different, but the problems we face financially when starting out in life are somehow similar: what do we do to start our lives on the right foot? Some of us are lucky to have money conversations with our families, but for most, that's not the case. Somehow, when it comes to money, society expects you to learn how to do everything right on your own.

This chapter is the missing guidebook on starting out in life.

The first thing you should do, as early as possible, is establish a banking relationship. Ideally, you would get a job in high school, then open a checking and savings account and be able to extend this relationship as needed.

How do you choose a bank? Or switch banks? If you already have a bank, it may be time to ask yourself if it's the best option for you.

First, you need to decide if you want to have a traditional bank or an online bank. My personal preference is to go with a traditional one. Yes, the interest you earn on money sitting in your checking or savings account is often higher with an online option, but when you have $500 or even $5,000 in savings, it does not make much difference. The convenience of a big bank-type branch at every corner might outweigh the extra few dollars you will earn in interest. As you become more financially stable and accumulate more money, opening an online savings account is a smart move.

You can check for the best interest rates offered on a website like Nerd Wallet.
https://www.nerdwallet.com/

If you go for a traditional bank, the second thing you will need to decide is what bank you would like to go with: a big bank like Wells Fargo or Bank of America, a local credit union, or something in between. Instead of giving you some generic advice like "consider all the factors," I will tell you what I like and why. I am a big bank type of person. I like to log into Wells Fargo and see all my accounts easily; I like to be able to get pretty much any product I want. Unlike my previous credit union, which was tied to a geographic region, I can find a Wells Fargo almost anywhere I go. And all my family has accounts with them, so transferring money between us is easy.

This is obviously not the answer for everyone. This is what works best for me, and it's not a perfect relationship. Recently, for the first time in 10 years, I had a very unpleasant situation to deal with. After much pain, they solved it, and we moved on.

Regardless of what you choose, try to open your own checking and savings account as soon as you can if you don't already have one.

Next on the agenda is getting a credit card. This is also something to do as soon as possible. The whole next chapter is about credit cards, but for now, I will just say that without a credit history and a credit score, you will have to jump through many more hoops in life.

The faster you start building your credit, the easier it will be for you down the road. I've heard it all: that participating in the credit game is a scam and you don't want to do it; that you never plan to buy anything major that needs to be financed; that you were just fine until now without credit, so why bother?

Well, for one, because if you want to sign a lease, get utilities or buy a cell phone, someone is going to want to check your credit rating. If you don't have one, you may not get the place you want or be approved for a cell phone. You may have to pay a deposit just to turn on your lights.

The easiest way to build credit is to get a credit card. You can also get a car loan and other debt, but that implies a repayment plan and some income. With a credit card, you can manage your cash flow, pay it off every month and build a nice credit history. Again, we will talk about this in depth in the next chapter.

Topic number three for today is signing a lease. If you want to move out, you will need to live somewhere. Assuming you are not moving into the home of a friend who does not care about your history because you have known each other for 20 years, signing a lease comes with a little bit of a headache and responsibility.

Here is what you must know:

- Consider getting some roommates when you first start out. It is good for your cash flow. The more roommates you have, the smaller the slice your housing costs take from your paycheck pie.

- Try to have as little baggage as possible: no prior evictions, no late rent payments, and no German shepherds. Yes, they are cute and smart, but many landlords can't have them because of their insurance policies.

- Think about the money you'll need to move in. Some places will ask for as much as the equivalent of two months' rent as a deposit, in addition to one month's rent up front. If your rent is $1,000 per month, that's $3,000 just to get your keys—without considering any moving costs. You can't just decide to move out today and be in tomorrow, in other words—you need to have some cash saved. If you plan on moving out, incorporate the total estimated amount into your budget and save for it. Once you're ready, start looking for a place about 30 days before you want to move.

- Think about the money you need to connect your utilities. Usually, if you have a good credit score and history, you can call the electrical, water, gas and internet companies and they will connect the utilities fast and easy. This is not the case, however, if you have a bad credit score or don't have a score at all. Don't worry, they will turn on your utilities—but it will require a deposit.

- If you don't have a stable income because you are in college, be prepared to have a cosigner. Your mom, grandma, Uncle Joe—someone with a job and stable income—may be needed. Personally, as the landlord of a house rented to students, I want someone I can go after if my house gets trashed. This is where roommates also come in handy: Jim may not be the first person you thought of as a roommate, but if his mom is willing to cosign for your place, Jim is your new friend.

The fourth and final thing I want to talk about some more is the idea I mentioned of having roommates. My personal recommendation is to have roommates as late in life as you can handle. For me, that was from 18 to 31. When I was 18, I had no choice; I was living in a dorm in college, and that was the deal. Later in life, I realized that spending as little money on housing as possible in our 20s makes sense. I didn't have any kids, and I spent lots of time hanging out with my friends anyways, so why not have some roommates?

When I was 26, my husband and I bought our first house. Did we really need 2,800 square feet, four bedrooms, three baths and two living rooms? No, we did not. We ended up owning a house and living for free because our roommates paid the mortgage.

At some point, you will outgrow roommates. But two or three years of splitting your most expensive cost with a few fun people will make it possible to save for other goals, be it travel, a down payment on a house or just to work less.

Once you move out on your own, be aware that costs have a way of piling up. Insurance, internet, food, rent; it's likely more than you had to pay before. Before you make this step, sit down and think about all the costs you will have and figure out if your income can support it.

To start your independent life without going into debt or adding stress to your life, make a plan.

My $.02

Do I go to graduate school as soon as I finish college, or should I work first?

Work first if you can, unless a career in your field is impossible without an advanced degree. One way you could get paid for graduate school is to work for a company that reimburses tuition. Not all companies do, but plenty will. For example, I did my MBA at night after work, and my employer picked up the bill. Most companies will want you to work for them for a few years if they pay for your school. Otherwise, they will make you pay it back when you quit.

Financially, the less you must pay for school and the faster you can start working, the better off you will probably be. Don't sign up for a master's degree in basket weaving because you can't think of something better to do. Join the Peace Corps. At least you won't accumulate more student loans while trying to figure out your life. Before you commit to an advanced degree, figure out if this is what you want to do, and need to do, to develop the career and life path you are planning to have.

How do I balance work and school?

I am a big fan of working early on in life. Yes, school is important, but I believe that we must also learn to deal with bosses we may not like and get experience to put on our resumes. Experience will increase your marketability and get you a job in your field faster than your GPA.

When does working not make any sense? Well, if you have an academic scholarship and are working at a minimum-wage job that doesn't leave you time to study and maintain the minimum GPA you need, then don't do it. If making $500 is going to cause you to lose $5,000 in scholarship money, then please put your time where it matters. But if you can do both, get a job.

While in school, should I continue to live at home or move into an apartment?

As exciting as moving out sounds, you are likely better off financially if you stay home for a little bit longer and save your money.

What if your generous parents are willing to pay for your apartment? Then it's up to you. Can you negotiate with them to get the money and start a business, go on a trip, invest, or anything else that you care more about instead? Then stay home and take advantage of the money.

Want to be the person with the apartment where everyone comes over to hang out every weekend? Move out.

Just remember it will be you cleaning up after they leave.

Your Bullet Point To-Do List

- If you are planning to move out soon, sit down and write out all the associated costs you can think of, both onetime expenses (like moving costs) and ongoing bills. If you do not know what to expect, ask around and figure it out. You do not want surprises.

- Now, compare those expenses to the cash you have saved and the income you have coming in every month. Can you afford to move out?

- If not, what do you need to save and how much more income per month do you need? Start saving and ask for a raise, then put a plan in place. Only then should you consider a move.

Chapter 3

My attempt to scare you into having a great credit score

"I am sorry, I can't marry you.

Your credit score sucks."

You know how you are told that your grades won't matter much after college? I kind of agree. They do matter when it comes to getting into graduate school, but once you graduate, who cares? Your boss does not.

But there is one grade everyone cares about for the rest of your life, and that is your credit score.

There are few things in your financial life as important as this number. If you are not one of those people who buys houses and cars with large stacks of cash, then one day, you will need your credit score. Heck, even if you do use cash for everything, including that house, you will still need a good credit score.

We touched on this in the previous chapter, but now let's dive in and see what this magical number is, where to get it from and what you can do when it's not that great.

Imagine that you have a credit score of 780 and your best buddy has a 650. What does that mean?

Let's say you need money for an emergency you did not foresee. You can go to the bank tomorrow and get a relatively low-interest, unsecured personal loan. You can get a credit card with a 21-month, zero-interest promotional offer to solve the problem for right now.

Your friend can't really do much. He may get a personal loan, but the interest rate will be ridiculous, and with his score, credit card companies are not tripping over themselves to extend promotional offers.

As you can see, a great credit score gives you options in life.

How about a house? Let's say you want to buy a condo in Los Angeles for $400k, with a mortgage at 3.75% interest and no down payment. This is a conversation for another time, I know. For now, just roll with my example, please. You are looking at a mortgage payment of around $1,850 per month in principal (paying back what you borrowed) and interest (the amount you've agreed to pay for the privilege of borrowing).

But with a credit score of 650, you will have a harder time finding a lender. Then you'll pay around 4.8%, with a payment of around $2,100—

an extra $250 per month for 30 years. That's lots of money. About $90k extra for the exact same house.

How much do you like that $90k? I like it a lot, so I am going to find a way to keep it for myself by having a good credit score.

Here are the things I want you to remember as you start to look into your credit score:

- There are three major credit bureaus that keep track of your score. Banks, credit card companies, cell phone companies, doctors' offices and any other businesses you might owe money to report how good you are with your bills to those three places. That's how you get a score. The bureaus are TransUnion, Equifax and Experian.

- FICO is not the fourth agency. Rather, it is an organization that uses information from the credit bureaus to come up with a number that many lenders use to decide how good you are likely to be at paying off your loans and credit cards. Each of the credit bureaus also assigns a score.

- There are many scores, and they are not the same. Why, you might wonder. Well, everyone needs to make money somehow. Most places used to charge big bucks to tell you your own credit score. Those days are gone. If you are paying to find out now, you are getting duped, because plenty of places will offer it to you for free.

Where are those places you speak about, Inga, where I can get my score? First, get a free Credit Karma account. You can get the TransUnion and Equifax numbers from them. It's a good start, but it's not the whole story. You are all giddy when you see 800 and head to the bank to get a new car loan, where they tell you your score is 740. You are like, "Whaaattttt? Credit Karma is a liar." Not quite, but unless you know what score your bank or lender uses, it is hard to know exactly what they will see. If you hate uncertainty and have control issues like I do, you can always call the bank to ask what they use and try to get that score to see where you stand.

- You can also get your FICO score from most banks and credit card companies for free. Log into your bank account or credit card account and do a search for FICO or credit score. There should be a link. Some of them don't update that often, so be aware that it may not be changing as fast as it should.

- There is a difference between your credit score and your credit report. You want both. The score is the number; the report is the dirty details. How many times you have been late, when you defaulted on your Comcast bill, things like that. Entries stay on your credit report for seven years for most stuff and 10 years for bankruptcies. After that, in most cases, they drop off, and we pretend like they never happened. There are situations, though, when old debt gets sold to new collection agencies and the clock starts ticking again.

What goes into your score?

- *Payment history*: how well you've paid your bills in the past. That accounts for about 30% of your grade. Big deal. Pay attention and don't be late. The later you are, the worse your score. Ninety days is worse than 30. No one knows if you are late for less than 30 days. You will still get a late payment fee from the credit card company, but it's unlikely the credit bureaus will be informed.

- *Credit utilization*: how much of your available credit you are using. This accounts for another 30% or so. If Capital One gave you a limit of $500 on your first credit card and you are using $480, you are way worse credit score-wise than Jimmy, who is using $25k of his $150k available credit. You are using 96% of your total credit availability ($480 of $500), and Jimmy is only using 16% ($25k of $150k), so he wins, even though it's ridiculous. It's a game. You need to know how to play it.

- *Length of credit history*: the average length of time you've had your accounts for. This accounts for about 15% of your total score. The "never close your old credit card accounts" rule plays into this one. The longer you have the accounts, the better your score will be. If you close an old credit card, you shorten the length of your credit history. That's why you often hear that you should never close your first card. When you close a card, you also decrease your total available credit, so your utilization ratio (see above) goes up. That's bad for your score.

- *Everything else*: First, there is the mix of credit or type of debt you have. Student loans, credit cards, car loans—the wider the mix, the better. Then, there is the amount of new credit you have. There is also some debate about whether the inquiries on your account matter. They might or might not; if they do, the impact is small. What I know for sure is that checking your credit score yourself will not affect you negatively. That's a soft inquiry. When you are shopping for debt like a new credit card, car loan or mortgage, those applications will appear on your report and are known as hard inquiries. Those probably will matter, in some small capacity.

Now that the boring stuff is out of the way, here is what I am excited about: things you can do to make your life better, credit-wise. Here are my top five things you need to know:

1. *You need to get on that credit-building bandwagon ASAP.*

Tammy, a very close friend of mine in college, is from Europe. She insisted that she was going back home as soon as she graduated, so she had no interest in this whole credit score nonsense. That all fell apart when Tammy fell in love and got married. Ten years later, she still lives in Florida. Do you think buying a car was easy for her when she decided she needed one to get to work?

We all know where this is going, so please, get some credit cards as soon as you can and start building a history, a report and a score. If you have nice parents or older siblings, ask them if you can be added as an authorized user to their accounts so you can piggyback on their good habits.

Note of caution: this plan is horrible if your brother spends his weekends taking cash advances from his credit cards and wasting it. Your joint score is only as good as the worst member of the party, so associate yourself only with responsible adults. And remember this rule when your little brother asks you to add him as an authorized user on your credit card.

2. *Try to train or retrain your brain to think of debt and credit cards as not that bad. They are good.*

You can use them for the sake of points and cash back. You can also get into debt and become really poor, really fast, if you decide to buy things you can't pay for. Choose who you want to be.

3. *Credit cards are also safer than the alternatives because you can always call and dispute a charge.*

Then it becomes someone else's problem to prove that a charge was *not* fraudulent. It's much harder to do with a debit card (although some banks now claim they do).

Here is a personal story: my husband travels a lot for work and once in a while, someone steals his credit card number. It's a pain because we then need to call and cancel the card and get a new one. But it is way less painful than the one time he used his debit card at an ATM in Mexico and then had $500 disappear every morning for the next few days, even after he called Wells Fargo and reported the problem.

With credit cards, the companies will immediately remove the charges and investigate the problem. With a debit card, the bank does a review; sometimes it takes a few days, and sometimes it takes a few weeks. Meanwhile, you may need this money for other purposes but can't use it. Things are changing but some banks still follow these rules.

4. *Credit cards offer many, many great benefits.*

Aside from any cash back, miles or other perks, you could have benefits such as extended warranties or travel protection. If you are not familiar with your card's benefits, Google it and see what perks you might qualify for. For example, you may also get car rental collision damage waivers and shopping discounts.

5. *The reality is that today's credit card landscape is overwhelming.*

There are so many cards and so many options. Nerd Wallet is a great site to use to compare them. https://www.nerdwallet.com/. You can find any card, with any perks you might want, under the credit card tab.

I am a big fan of using credit cards because why would you not? If you are responsible and don't buy things you can't afford, then using a credit card will give you points or cash back. In my opinion, cashback is better than points because it gives you more flexibility. But if you find yourself traveling all the time on the same airline or want to finance your vacation with points, travel reward cards are good too.

"That's all great, Inga, but what can I do if my credit is not good? Can it be fixed?" Yes, it can.

Any score can be fixed and improved. First, figure out why your score is low. Is it because you are spending too much money on your credit cards? Remember, a big part of your score is how much you have charged on your card compared to how much total available credit you have.

This is the easiest problem to fix.

#1: Stop using your card!
#2: Pay off your balance!

Putting together a plan to get out of credit card debt is very important. You can either attack the card with the smallest balance first or the one with the highest interest rate.

If, however, the problem is late payments or even collections, then there is more work to do.

Generally, first, try to pay off the debt. A paid debt is usually better than an unpaid one, especially if it is recent. Then, write a letter to the company that reported you and nicely ask for the late payment/collections to be removed because you fixed the problem. If you can give them a good reason why you did not pay your bill on time, even better. Some words of caution: if the amount to be paid is large and the debt is old, you need to evaluate what makes more sense. I am not telling you not to pay your debt, but in some cases, you really need to decide if it is worth it. This is where paying for professional help will pay off.

My $.02

How many credit cards should I have? Can I have too many or not enough cards?

There is no correct number. If you Google this, you will get 1,597 opinions. (Yes, I made up this number.) I go with the idea that three to five is just fine. If you need more (and need is a relative term), go for it. Some people are into travel hacking (when you get free flights and hotels by signing up for a new card and using the free points the card offers). Others like to always be on the hunt for new deals. I don't. I like simplicity: having one card for myself and one for my business works just fine for me.

If you have consolidated finances with a spouse or partner, you may decide to each have a card. With some of my clients who need help spending less, we usually put together a system where the budgeted items go on one credit card, and anything above that goes on a different one. Side note: for people who are in debt and have issues sticking to a budget, we cut up all credit cards and only use debit cards. Until spending is under control, credit cards are off limits, no matter how good those points are.

Again, I don't think there is a magical number. More than one and less than six is a good rule of thumb to follow.

Does closing cards hurt your credit?

Yes, it does. Okay, mostly it does.

But, as with everything else, think about your own situation. Why do you want to close the card? Is it because you have too many accounts and can't keep them straight? Is it because you don't trust yourself with a Macy's card in the store? Is it because you don't want to pay the $95 yearly fee on some airline card you never use? If your goal is not to use them, find a way to do so without impacting your credit score. Rather than closing cards, consider shredding them. Shredding won't help with your yearly fee, though, so in a situation like that, closing the account may be justified.

What do you think about store cards?

I get asked about this all the time. Personally, I am not a fan. Does anyone really need a Victoria's Secret credit card? Maybe if you make a living being clothed in Victoria's Secret, then you do, but most of us do not. Yes, there are perks, but the more I ask around, the more I see how we tend to buy more just because we have the card. That's not going to make our financial life any better.

They do have one great benefit, though. They are easier to get than the major cards (Visa, MasterCard, American Express or Discover) and can be used to start rebuilding your credit history if things went wrong at some point.

Do I have any store cards? I do have one. And that is with Home Depot. Last summer I financed kitchen cabinets from Home Depot with a 0% APR* for 24 months.

If you can pay no interest for two years and invest that money somewhere else, making even the 1% some savings accounts are offering, why wouldn't you? Same goes for Best Buy cards, furniture store cards and the like. As with everything else, there is a good use and a bad use of store credit cards. Signing up for every card under the sun to get 10% off on your $50 purchase is probably not the best idea. Signing up for the Home Depot card to get $1,000 off your $10,000 cabinets might be.

*Sorry, jargon alert: annual percentage rate.

How do I get a perfect credit score?

Who cares?! No one is going to give you brownie points for a perfect credit score. There is no MVP wall out there with names. Get to a score of 780 to 800, get the best available rates and move on to a worthier task in life.

Your Bullet Point To-Do List

- Go to annualcreditreport.com and pull your credit reports from all three agencies. You will need to fill out a form and decide which report you want. You can only get each of the three reports free once a year. If you need some more help, Mary Beth Storjohann has a very good chapter in her book *Work Your Wealth: 9 Steps to Making Smarter Choices with Your Money* on dissecting your credit score and what to look for to find errors.

- Use your credit card or bank to get your credit score.

- Sign up for a Credit Karma account, install the app on your phone and go wild. It will update once a week—enjoy the changes.

- For bonus points: calculate your utilization ratio by adding up all the debt you currently have on all your credit cards and dividing it by the total available limit. For example, if I have one credit card with a $1,000 limit (money I can spend), and I've spent $300 on it, my utilization ratio is 300/1000 = 30%. Work on getting your ratio under 30% for each of your cards.

Chapter 4

Why are we obsessed with paying off debt?

How rethinking your plan can make you richer

Most of us have a burning desire to get rid of debt. But is it optimal from a financial perspective?

If you have a great credit score, you can get car loans and mortgages cheaply these days. Why would you want to pay off a car loan at 2% when you can invest that money and make at least 3% or 4%? If your alternatives are to either pay off your debt or spend the money on lifestyle expenses, it's a good idea to pay off the debt—at least you'll have some something to show for it. But if your choices are to pay off debt or invest and build wealth, think twice.

Here is a real-life example.

Imagine you have a $400k mortgage with 20 years to go before it's paid off, a $20k car loan with five years to go and about $20k in student loans with 10 years to go. Let's say your mortgage is at 4.25%, your car is at 1%, and your student loans are at 4%, all realistic given our current interest rate environment.

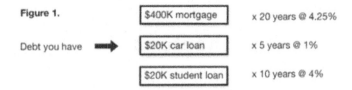

Figure 1.

Debt you have ➡

$400K mortgage	x 20 years @ 4.25%
$20K car loan	x 5 years @ 1%
$20K student loan	x 10 years @ 4%

Let's also imagine that you have an extra $200 per month to do whatever you want with. Now, imagine that you have the following three choices. Here is a picture to make it easier to visualize:

Figure 2.

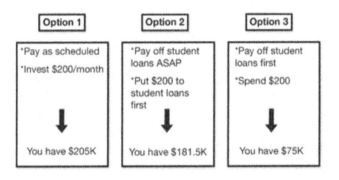

Option 1	Option 2	Option 3
*Pay as scheduled *Invest $200/month ⬇ You have $205K	*Pay off student loans ASAP *Put $200 to student loans first ⬇ You have $181.5K	*Pay off student loans first *Spend $200 ⬇ You have $75K

1. Pay off the debt as scheduled. (Make no extra payments.) Invest the $200 each month for the next 20 years. After you pay off the car in five years, also invest the $345 you just freed up; add $200 per month in 10 years after you pay off the student loans. In other words, all your extra money always goes to investments.

2. Pay off your student loans ASAP, since the interest rate is four times as high as your car

loan. Let's put the extra $200 we have available into it too until the loans are paid off. The car loan will be gone at much the same time as you finish paying off the student loans. Once you are done with the loans, put all the extra money towards the house until it is paid off as well. After everything is paid off, invest the extra money.

3. Finally, let's be realistic. Most people do not have the self-discipline to put everything into paying off debt, so instead of investing the $200 right now, we will spend it on stuff. Everything else is still the same as in #2.

Which of the three scenarios would you prefer?

Here is what would happen in each case:

1. After 20 years, you will be debt free. If we assume a return of 5% on your investments, in addition to having no debt, you will also have about $205k in investment savings.

2. At the end of 20 years, you will still be debt free and you will also have about $181.5k available. Just to be sure we are clear, that is $23,500 less than in scenario #1.

3. Finally, let's be human and spend the $200 on vacations, eating out and pedicures. In 20 years, we will be done with all debt (in 18 years, actually) and have about $75k in our hands.

Do you see the problem? Let's think about this. Let's say you are 30 right now. In 20 years, you will probably still be working. So why in the world would you pay off the debt faster? If you are 20, the situation and the numbers become so much bigger and you are even more better off not prepaying your debt.

As you look at yourself in the future, you are debt free no matter which path you take, but you can have an extra $23.5k in assets if you stop rushing to prepay your debt. And I assumed a 5% investment return rate. If I run the numbers with 6% or 7%, the difference becomes even greater.

Many of us are opposed to being in debt and I am no exception. Despite the logical arguments I can frame for others, on some instinctive level, I do not like debt. And yet I am trying to convince you that the way we approach debt and the idea of debt may not be financially optimal.

As I read personal finance books and my students' essays about their financial futures, I see the same trend and the same ideas: people do not like debt. My students want to pay off their cars, their credit cards, and their mortgages.

I know what the textbooks tell you about mortgages and student loans being good debt and credit cards being bad debt, but now I want you to take it a step further.

What is good debt? It is debt that makes your life better. Does a mortgage make your life better?

Maybe. If you have a house you love that is not stressing you out financially, then I would say that debt is good. However, if you, like one of my students, just took out $200k in student loans to get a degree in film and then realized you really won't be doing anything with it, I am sure you feel bad about that debt, no matter how many times the textbook tells you student loans are good.

I would also divide debt into two tiers: daily life debt and debt that improves your financial situation by helping you accumulate wealth.

For those of you who have not gone into debt yet: the less daily life debt you take on, the less stressed you will be. This applies to things like going out to dinner and putting it on your credit card or going to Nordstrom, spending a whole bunch of money on things to make yourself feel better, and then not knowing how to pay off that credit card. For the people who are already there, as I mentioned in the last chapter, stop using the cards first and then put together a plan for paying off the debt. There is no point in trying to dig yourself out of debt while buying another food processor.

However, once you get rid of your credit card debt, think about how to use debt to advance your life. And this is where I am going to tell you to wait before you pay off the car loan, mortgage, or student loan that may have an interest rate that is too low to justify paying it off.

I am good at telling others what to do, but to make this a fair game, I also need to tell you what's going on in my family. My husband and I have slightly different ideas on debt. When in doubt, I err on the side of cash hoarding and piling up investments. He likes paying off debt. When there is more than one person to consider, you need to look at the non-financial aspects of your decisions as well. Do we invest, or do we pay off debt? We found a compromise, or what I think of as doing both.

First, we maximize our retirement accounts. Next, we decide how much to save in the brokerage account for all kinds of future goals. Finally, we decide how much extra we should put into any debt.

I have some student loans at about 2.5%. For the longest time, I was not paying them off aggressively—because why would I? We had other, higher-interest consumer debt. Now, however, after saving and investing, we decided to accelerate the payment on those loans to potentially prepare ourselves for a future with smaller incomes due to a job change.

We also agreed to pay extra on a mortgage we have for an investment property. This was purely a comfort decision. We would like to pay off that house and free up the mortgage for different purposes. Is this the best financial decision? Who knows. I can find a few reasons why it's not, but it is what works best for us, and that's just fine. You do not have to maximize every dollar every time. Sometimes, it is about other things, like going on a vacation, buying that ridiculously expensive bottle of wine or making your spouse happy. Emotions drive human decision-making, and it's okay to do what makes you happy.

When it comes to money, there is always a psychological aspect to consider. The peace of mind that comes with not having any debt may be worth way more than any rate of return. As long as you have considered both angles, it is okay to decide to pay it off. What I want you to think through is, does it make sense for you? For your personal situation?

My $.02

Paying off debt and saving money: how do I juggle both?

Put together a budget! Everything in life starts with a cash flow map. My personal view is that you should pay off debt and build a cushy stash of dollars at the same time. You do not want to be the person who puts every dollar into her mortgage and can't come up with $500 to fix the car.

Rule number one: make sure you have some emergency savings. I know that financial planners tell you that the equivalent of six months of expenses is the right amount for an emergency fund, but I hate rules that are supposed to fit everyone. (They never do.) Look at your situation and the cash you can access if needed. Then, decide how much will make you comfortable and keep it on hand. I personally like the number $3,000. It is completely arbitrary but I feel that having $3k in your savings account makes you feel like you are covered when an unexpected expense shows up. Come up with your number now!

Once the emergency savings is in your account, decide how much extra you want to deploy to debt versus investments. My break-even point for long-term investments is around 6%. In other words, if I have any debt above 6%, I focus on it. If I have debt below 6%, I will invest and maybe pay some extra towards the principal, maybe not.

Although these are two separate rates, one for debt and one for investments, in the end, they are both just ways to use our money. Compare what you would earn if you invest versus what you will pay if you don't repay your debt and decide on what makes more sense.

That said, there is something psychologically pleasing about paying off more of your debt than you should. If you get a kick out of that, fine—put an extra $100 or $200 into your car payment.

I need cash. What do I do?

Do you have a wealthy grandma? That would be ideal. No? Me neither. Well, how good is your credit score? If it's great, then you are probably set. Yes, you need to have an emergency fund. I am all about that, but at the same time, if you have a credit score of 800 and can always access a 0% card or a cheap personal loan, you have more cash available than someone with a score of 650. Or, if you have a car that is paid off, you can take a car loan against it. In other words, go to the bank and tell them you have a paid-off car and need to finance it. It is like getting a car loan with the car as the collateral, so if you do not pay your loan, the bank takes away your car. As you can see, there are options.

Your Bullet Point To-Do List

- Write down all the debt you have, including the monthly minimum payment and the interest rate for each account.

- Write down how much you are contributing to savings, retirement and investments—anything you are putting away somewhere for the future.

- Think about potential scenarios. If you have a little bit of extra cash, what can you do with it? Imagine and write down as many scenarios as possible. For example, the extra $100 per month can go to student loans, your mortgage or your retirement or brokerage account. Or maybe you want to save it for your backpacking trip to Asia. You might need to enlist someone's help, but the more you think about this yourself, the better. Then, decide which of those paths you would like to take. Come back and reconsider your options every few months.

PART II:
MOVING UP IN LIFE

Chapter 5

You can be an investment genius too

Let's do this right

True story: I graduated with a degree in finance and no idea how to invest my money. I didn't have much money, so it didn't really bother me. Then, I got an MBA and still nada. At the end of my MBA, it occurred to me that, with a few investment classes behind me, no one had yet talked about where to go and what buttons to press—to, you know, invest. I knew plenty about the efficient market hypothesis, the types of investments and the types of accounts. I was textbook set. But I really had no idea how to take that knowledge and translate it into investments. There I was, 24 years old, with a finance degree, an MBA and nothing but As in investment classes—and literally no knowledge of basics like how and where to open an account.

A relative of mine, someone who is very intelligent and plenty educated, told me that for her, investing is associated with fear. She is afraid of investing money.

It's not an uncommon feeling, partly because of all the jargon used in the financial industry.

My goal for this chapter is to talk about investments a little differently, so there is no intimidation around this topic—to make it all as commonsense as possible. The process will consist of five steps. Here is a flowchart to make it easier to visualize:

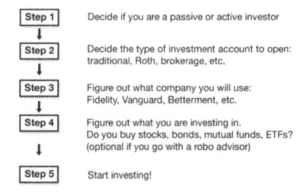

The Five Step Investment Process

Step 1 — Decide if you are a passive or active investor

Step 2 — Decide the type of investment account to open: traditional, Roth, brokerage, etc.

Step 3 — Figure out what company you will use: Fidelity, Vanguard, Betterment, etc.

Step 4 — Figure out what you are investing in. Do you buy stocks, bonds, mutual funds, ETFs? (optional if you go with a robo advisor)

Step 5 — Start investing!

Let's start with the two big ideas about how people invest.

Step 1: Figure out your investment philosophy.[1]

There are two main investment philosophies out there: active and passive.

People who believe in active managers try to outperform a benchmark such as the S&P 500

---

[1] Some of this information originally appeared on my website, attainablewealthfp.com.

index (a selection of 500 large company stocks designed to gauge the return performance of the entire US stock market).

Passive managers invest with the market. They accept the returns of the market because they believe that overall, markets are efficient and it's extremely difficult to do better than the Borg or whatever the common element is in *The Matrix*.

I spent years reading academic papers on investments. Although there certainly are arguments for active management (for example, in bad times, active management can beat passive investing), I will sum up the research in one sentence.

Active management is expensive.

This usually translates into lower returns for investors. Few funds (and fund managers) produce returns that outpace their costs. More importantly, it is almost impossible to consistently identify the ones that do. Also, most of the amazing returns come from hedge funds or private funds and they don't really care about your $250. If you do not have big money, you have a tough time even getting access to good active investment advice.

Thus, I am a big believer in investing passively. It's not that I don't think an individual can do better than a specific benchmark. We do find people who do, but we find them after the fact, with no guarantee that their success will continue.

What this really means for you is that your best bet is to buy a little bit of everything and wait. In finance jargon, this is known as building a well-diversified portfolio and investing for the long term. Let it grow and don't bother much.

I am obviously making it all way too simplistic and personally, I did take active positions in the past, but this is how I would explain it to my grandma if she were into investing. For now, it really is all you need to know to be a successful long-term investor.

Step 2: Figure out what type of investment account you want or need to open.

This is completely independent of the investment philosophy discussion above. There are many types of accounts out there, and I am going to mention the most common ones. Primarily, there are retirement-type accounts, taxable investment accounts (known as brokerage accounts) and education-related accounts.

One thing I want to make sure you're clear on relates to the difference between work/job/employer-sponsored retirement accounts and individual retirement accounts.

Employer-Sponsored Retirement Accounts

When you get a job, your employer might have a plan set up in which you can participate. It might also have a company match, which means that for every dollar you save, your employer contributes some amount.

The most common of these retirement accounts is the 401(k), but there are also 403(b), 457 and SIMPLE IRA accounts, among others.

Here are a few things you'll need to know to sound like "you a pro" at your next company orientation:

- A contribution match is a company benefit you should consider in addition to your salary because—unless you blow it by not contributing to your retirement plan—it translates into extra income. The money you save in a retirement plan is called a contribution. There are lots of different ways that companies approach this, but a 3% match is pretty standard. A 3% one-to-one match means that if you contribute 3% of your salary to the 401(k), the company will put in the same amount and you will end up with 6% of your salary in your retirement savings. Good deal. I have friends with 15% matches, but that's just crazy. If you can get a job like that, it's an amazing benefit. Sometimes, you will hear of a match that works like this: the employer contributes 100% of the first 3% and 50% of the next 2%. This means that if you put in 5% of your salary, the company will put in 4% and you will end up with 9%.

- Vesting refers to the time required for you to keep the employer match. Companies usually give you the match contributions each pay period you work for them, but if you quit before the official vesting, they will take their money back. It's sad. A three-year vesting period is common. A 20/40/60/80/100% vesting over five years is also something you see a lot of—if you quit after three years, you get to keep 60% of the money the company gave you, etc.

- Should I participate? If there is a match, yes, you should. Free money, free money. You should contribute up to the match no matter what. Above that? Well, it depends. In a few chapters, I will send you to a financial planner to get this type of specific question answered. But if there is a match, contribute at least that amount, please. If I ever dated a guy who told me he did not have money for his 401(k) and was losing the match, I would immediately say, "It's not happening, buddy. You can't be trusted to make sound life decisions." Add that to your Tinder application. You can thank me later.

You-Sponsored Retirement Accounts

What can you do if your job does not offer a retirement plan, or if there is no match and the company plan is not that good (the investment options all have ridiculously high fees) or if you just want to be the most prepared-for-retirement 22-year-old I know?

Look at individual retirement accounts, also known as IRAs. There are two types: traditional and Roth.

With the traditional version, you pay less in taxes now when you put the money into the account, but pay tax on it when you take it out at retirement. For example, if you make $30k per year and contribute $5k to your IRA, you will only pay taxes on $25k now. The max you can put in is $5,500 if you are young and $6,500 if you are old. The IRS defines anyone 50 or older as old. That's their definition. Not mine.

A Roth is the opposite. You don't save anything on taxes now but will not pay any taxes in the future. The $5k contribution you put in does not do anything for your taxes this year, but it will grow for many, many years. Then when you take all those millions out, they will be tax free.

I am a big fan of the Roth. The sad thing is that I never had a Roth because I missed that boat. By the time I realized it's a great way to stash some money away, I was making too much to qualify. Again, according to the IRS's definition, not mine. The Roth has what is known as phase-outs, or income limits. If you are above it, you can't contribute. The limits change all the time, and the IRS website is a great place to find up-to-date information. You might be surprised, but the website is very well written, easy to follow and has everything you need.

There is also a great comparison of the two types of IRAs. Check it out at https://www.irs.gov/retirement-plans/traditional-and-roth-iras.

One more reason I like the idea of a Roth is that you can take out the money you've invested. Most retirement plans have a penalty of 10% on early withdrawals, although there are exceptions. The Roth does not.

You will be penalized on any growth (investment or interest returns on your contributions) you take out before you are 59.5 years old, but whatever you put in is your money to take out, whenever you want. That does not mean that you *should* take it out, but theoretically, you could.

That makes the Roth a good way to have a backup for needs other than retirement, like sending your kids to college or a "vacay." (I hope you know I am joking about the last one.)

That's everything you need to know about retirement accounts for now.

Taxable Brokerage Accounts

Let's move on to brokerage accounts. This is money that you invest after tax (that is, you've already been taxed on it), so there is no tax-savings incentive—money that can grow for any goal you might have or just because. Whenever you sell any of your investments, you will have to pay taxes on the growth (anything above what you put in). How can you use it? Pretty much for everything. These accounts are a good way to put money aside, invest it, and see it grow over the long term. The investment choices in the brokerage accounts are pretty much the same as in the traditional or Roth IRAs. The big difference is that there is no tax incentive, now or later, but you always have access to the money.

Education Accounts

Many students ask me about 529 accounts. These are also investment accounts, but they are a special type that can be used to pay for college. By the time you are in college, it is too late to set one up. The whole point of them is to put a little money in early on, let it grow and then use it for college later. This type of account is great for parents to set up for their children.

Every state has one. Some offer tax incentives at the state level if you invest in one (like NY or PA) and some do not (like the great state of CA). There is lots of debate in the financial planning world about whether these are good accounts.

I personally like them, if:

- you open one early in the child's life,
- fund it to the best of your ability (and not at the detriment of your retirement), and then
- use the money and all the growth (that's the appeal) tax free, for tuition, room and board, study abroad, etc., 10 to 18 years down the road.

I opened one for my son when he was three weeks old. I have no clue how much college is going to cost in 18 years, if he is going to be the next

Einstein and will get a full ride, or if he will even go to college.

The bottom line is that I am doing my best with available cash. My goal is to fund the 529 account for a few years and then stop and let it grow. The sooner you start putting money into it, the less you must put in, as the time between your contributions and when the child is 18 and goes to college works in your favor.

This is how the money grows. I also tell my clients that they should open these accounts after they take care of about eight other things. This is not priority number one or even number three, by any means. Pay off your consumer debt, save for retirement, enjoy your life, and then open a 529 account. But, if paying for your kid's college is high up on your priority list, then look into these accounts sooner rather than later.

This list is by no means exhaustive, but I hope it gives you enough of an overview of investment accounts before we move on.

Step 3: Figure out what company you will use to open your account.

I don't know why textbooks still insist on telling us the difference between full brokers and discount brokers. These days, we are all pretty much working in the discount broker world unless someone is managing our money. So instead of focusing on that, I will focus on the difference between do-it-yourself places like Fidelity,

Vanguard, E*Trade, or Schwab (the ones I called the "old-fashioned companies") and robo-advisers, which are companies that invest your money by using computer programs to do most of the work.

The first decision you need to make is if you'll go to a company where you pick your investments and make a few decisions (which I will be referring to as the first bunch) or to a robo-adviser (second bunch) where you pretty much make one decision.

A robo-adviser is an investment company, just like Fidelity or TIAA or Vanguard. I am going to push for the robo-advisers because I do not think you can do better on your own unless you have specialized investment skills, and the costs of robos are attractively low. I also think their costs are justified for the value they provide.

Once you decide on the path, decide on which company you want to go to.

For me, it comes down to fees and other costs.

For the first bunch (the old-fashioned companies), you need to see what the trade fees are; in other words: how much does the company charge you every time you buy or sell something? You're going to find prices around $4.95 to $9.99. Most of these places will also let you buy their own funds for free. For example, Vanguard will waive the fee when you buy Vanguard funds, Fidelity will do the same for Fidelity funds, etc. There is not much difference between them. Cost-wise, if you are investing for the long term, you are not going to buy and sell that often, so $4.99 versus $7.99 does not make such a big difference. So, any of those companies is just fine.

If you are already used to a company because that's where your 401(k) is, go with that one. If not, it's your choice. I like the Fidelity interface and research tools myself.

For the second bunch, the robo-advisers, you will pay a percentage of your assets (the amount of money in your account) rather than trade fees.

The big players as I am writing this book are Betterment (my favorite), and Wealthfront https://www.betterment.com/ and https://www.wealthfront.com.

They both charge 0.25% for their basic accounts. They offer pretty much the same services. The only decision you need to make is what percentage of your investments to put into stocks and what percentage to put into bonds, and they will do the rest of the work for you. Just like TurboTax, if you have no idea what to do, they will ask you a few questions and offer some suggestions how to decide no that stock to bond split.

Step 4: What exactly am I investing in?

"Hold on, lady," you may be saying to yourself, "you did not explain stocks versus bonds."

Here is my cocktail party explanation. When you buy stocks, you buy a little slice of the company.

You own it. Let's be serious—our small investments don't give us much power, but if you really wanted to, you could vote and participate in company decisions. You also have no idea how much money you will make on these stocks. When you sell, you will get some money back: it could be more than what you paid for it, but it could also be less. No one knows, but if the company is doing well and the overall market isn't crashing, you can reasonably expect to get more. Additionally, some companies pay what are known as quarterly dividends—a percentage of profits to them, extra money for you—once every three months, to sweeten the deal. The higher the dividends and the higher the price of the stock when you sell compared to when you bought, the richer you get.

Bonds, on the other hand, are like loans you make to a company or government. Every so often, they will pay you interest, and at the end, when the bond-loan is over, you will get your original investment back. For example, if it is a five-year bond, then you will get your money back after five years. There is less risk than in stock investments, but you could still lose money if the company or government goes bankrupt. You could also lose if interest rates go up and you need to sell the bond before the loan is over (before those five years are up). Just trust me on this last one as there is a long explanation for why interest rates affect bond prices the way they do.

You hear the words "diversified portfolio" a lot. Okay, maybe you don't, but I do. This means "Don't put all your eggs in one basket." In other words, don't put all your money into one stock because you think it's a great company. It may be great, but if things don't pan out well, all your wealth will be gone, and you will be crying. Instead, put money into different "asset classes" or baskets: stocks, bonds, real estate, some international stuff. There are plenty of funds available in each of these categories. A little bit of everything goes a long way.

It is very hard to build a good portfolio if you buy individual companies and don't know what you are doing. You need to buy lots and lots of companies to spread your risk, so most common folk, like me, invest in something called mutual funds, index funds or exchange-traded funds (ETFs). The idea behind them is pretty much the same: get a whole bunch of stocks, bonds or other assets together and then sell the whole pie to people in small slices.

There are plenty of differences between them, but the point of this book is explaining the big-picture concepts. An investment textbook (or Google) will tell you exactly what the differences are if you care to get into more detail.

One of the significant differences between these investments I do need to mention is cost. When I talk about cost, by the way, I am not talking about the price of one unit, but the fees and other costs the fund manager charges you for the privilege of owning the fund. A fund could cost $10,000 per unit but be cheap because its annual fees are 0.025% of your total investment, or cost $10 per unit, but be expensive because its fees are 3.5% of your investment.

It used to be that mutual funds were expensive and ETFs and index funds were cheap. I can no longer make this statement in 2017. But if you go back to the beginning of this chapter, you will remember my love affair with passive investing. In other words, I am a cheapo when it comes to investments, and I go for index funds from companies like Vanguard and Schwab that are just fine for my long-term investment purposes.

If you got anything from the previous page, I hope it is that investing is not that easy if you don't know the basics. That's why I encourage you to go to a robo-adviser and let them do the work for you.

Asset allocation (how you split your money between bonds and stocks to create a diversified portfolio) is still very important. Over the long term, it is much more important than the individual investments you buy.

You are responsible for that decision, but at a robo-adviser, at least you need to make just one decision and not 100.

Fewer decisions, less chance to screw up. Why complicate our lives?

Step 5: Now, make it happen

Okay, so you've decided that you will either go a robo-advisor or do it yourself with a company like Fidelity or Vanguard. What do you do now?

Go to the company's website, click on Open an Account or Start Investing Now and follow the prompts. You will need to validate your Social Security number, supply some info and link your bank account so money can go in and out for investments.

In a few days or hours, you will be in business.

Before you invest your rent money in the next Apple stock, though, I would like to encourage you to play with some fake money and get a better sense of what this investment world is about, especially if you are going to build your own investment account (aka gambling with individual companies).

There are lots of tools out there but here is one you could use: http://www.cboe.com/trading-tools/virtual-trading-tools/virtual-trade.

You can pretend you are a trader for a few days or a week, get comfortable and then go from there to a real investment company. But keep in mind that a lot of the times when newish investors think they're doing well, it's just that the overall stock market is doing well or because they hit a lucky streak in a particular investment. Only time will tell.

I used to invest in individual companies because it's fun and I thought I was quite good at it. I even followed companies, waited for their quarterly reports, and traded on that info. Guess what? I wasn't better than the market, after all. I wasn't bad, but for every huge gain, I also had a loss. I did about as well as the market, but it required a lot of work on my part.

Now I log into my account, spend some time looking around and then go to the beach. I learned my lesson: even when you have the skills and knowledge to invest actively, it may not be worth it.

My $.02

Are target retirement funds a good way to invest?

When you start your 401(k), almost every company will offer something called target retirement date or lifecycle funds. These funds match your investments to your retirement date. For example, a target date fund 2055 means that you will retire in 2055 (many years to go), which translates into being able to take lots of investment risk and invest mostly in stocks.

What do I think of these very popular funds? Frankly, they are better than nothing. It is great if you have no idea what to do or don't want to spend the time on your 401(k). I am not the biggest fan, however, just because I can usually build my own target-date fund for a lower price. But this is not true for everyone. If the idea of choosing investments or contacting a financial planner to help you (more on this in a later chapter) makes you a little queasy, fine, go for the target date funds. It is certainly better than not investing at all. Just be aware that some of them come with a pretty steep price. The higher the price, the less money you keep for yourself.

How do you overcome a fear of investing?

Back to this question. The best thing to do is to meet with someone who has more knowledge and can explain investing to you simply. Usually, that someone is a financial planner. There is a whole chapter on this later. An hour or two will get you more comfortable with how this world works.

You do need to realize that losing money is inevitable if you invest in the stock market through any type of account. How much and when you lose it is unknowable, but the fact that you will at some point is certain. What's important to realize, though, is that over the long term (and I am talking 10+ years), you will probably (as I am not allowed to offer any certainties) make money. I personally think you will make money, but no one can promise you anything, so that's not a fact, just a strong belief based on the history of the financial markets over the last 80 years.

Another thing to realize is that if you go with a robo-adviser, there is not much you can mess up. Same goes for your 401(k). In either case, you are still investing the market so you could lose money at one point. But remember, if you do not sell when the market is down, your loss is imaginary. If you do panic and sell, you make it real.

Are there bad investments out there? How can I spot the scams?

There are so many bad investments out there, I want to weep. I see clients every day who own junk investments I don't know how to unload because they come with steep penalties.

For example, when you buy annuities in your 403(b), which is very typical for teachers, you might pay steep penalties if you want to get out of them before a specific number of years. If you decide to move your money into a different investment, you may lose as much as 10% to 20%.

If anyone is promising or guaranteeing you a specific return, I would be very skeptical. How can someone know what the markets will return in the future?

Other things to turn your nose up at: anyone trying to sell you a whole life insurance policy (more on that later) when you don't need one—or anything at all that can't be explained to you in very simple terms.

People who try to appear knowledgeable while making you feel stupid are to be avoided. They may not be scammers, but if they can't be completely transparent, they may be trying to rip you off. Or—almost as bad—they may not even know what they are trying to sell you.

How much should you invest in a 401(k) at different ages?

This is the million-dollar question that no one can answer for you unless they first talk to you about your goals and the future you want.

How and where do you want to retire? When? Doing what? This question requires analysis because you might be okay with very little money or you might need lots of it. How much you should save in your 401(k) depends on about a hundred factors. By the way, the useless textbook answer is

10% if you start at age 25, but that is too universal to apply to all of us.

Bottom line? As much as I want to answer this question, I can't. My best advice is to save as much as you can until you can sit down with a financial planner to calculate an accurate figure for you.

Your Bullet Point To-Do List

- If you have a job, figure out if it has a 401(k) and if it offers a match. If it does and you are not contributing yet, make sure you change that right now. Take that match.

- If your job is not offering a retirement plan and you do have a job (income to show on your taxes), consider opening either a traditional IRA or a Roth IRA. Even a tiny contribution is a good start for your future.

- Put together a plan on how and when you will increase your contributions to your 401(k) or IRA. For example, if you started with $20 per month now, when will you go to $30? How about $100?

Chapter 6

Who said insurance is not fun?

Or, why I refer to my child as the $15 baby

Let's be serious: talking about insurance is as exciting as watching paint dry. I considered not having a chapter about this because I feel your pain. But we are all responsible adults here, so let's adult and talk about insurance. I have seen too many clients and family members who didn't have insurance at a time they desperately needed it.

Let's get started with a story about health insurance before we explore the different types of insurance out there.

At a hospital birth class, I talked to another lady about the upcoming bills associated with having a baby. As you can see, I like accosting strangers and asking them personal money questions. Even though we had babies at the same hospital, almost at the same time, and got the same care, our babies cost us significantly different amounts of money.

The difference comes from two sources: how much we each pay per month in health insurance premiums and the copays and deductibles associated with our plans when we actually had babies. Both of those are driven by our employers' rules.

It's a very unfair world. While she pays a few hundred dollars each month for her family's premiums and also had to pay $3k out of pocket to have the baby, I don't pay anything to cover my entire family. My baby cost me a whopping $15, in total, from the second I found out I was pregnant until now, when he is over a year old.

I am giving you this example so you do not rely on conversations with your friends about copays and deductibles. Even if you have the same insurance company, unless you both work for the same employer under the same plan, "results may vary." Dramatically.

As you look for jobs or compare offers, consider the medical premiums and coverage as significant as your salary. That $500 monthly pay increase at your new job is worse than useless if you pay an extra $700 for health benefits for your family.

So let's start the insurance conversation with more on health insurance. Oh, the pain of not having good health insurance. You don't realize how important it is until you must start paying for it. If you are under a certain age (usually 26), you will be covered by your parents, assuming your parents have insurance and love you enough to keep paying for you. If you don't, then you must get your own coverage, and it could easily run you a few hundred dollars per month for thin coverage. If you don't buy it, you will be penalized by the government.

There is not much wisdom I can give you on this one except to find a job that has excellent benefits, if you are the type of person who is into jobs, or to get a spouse with a great plan that will cover you too.

As mentioned, not all plans are the same, even those from the same company. Kaiser, my health insurance plan, is what's known as an HMO plan, which means you must go to their doctors, unlike PPO plans, where you can choose among many doctors.

In addition to the health maintenance organization (HMO) and preferred provider organization (PPO) plans, high-deductible health plans (HDHPs) are popular these days. You need to know what they are.

I am a big fan of HDHPs for young, healthy people. If you have diabetes, this plan is not for you. But if you go to the doctor once in a while, a high-deductible plan may work very well. Your out-of-pocket cost is high, but in many cases, your employer will contribute to a health savings account (HSA) and fund some of that deductible. You also contribute through payroll deductions, tax free, and in a few months or a year, you may have enough to cover the entire deductible.

If you don't use the money, it just keeps growing and being invested until you need it. One day, you may end up with another stash of money you didn't even know you had.

The drawback is that something might happen to you that is not too major—I am not talking a heart attack, more like a ruptured appendix—when you do not have enough money in your HSA. When you must pay $6k for surgery out of pocket, and you don't have the money, it's a big deal. If you have a choice, it's a risk you'll have to balance against the advantages of lower premiums.

The final and completely unrelated words of advice are—and remember I am not a doctor—that, from a financial point of view, it's better to go to an urgent care center than an emergency room if you don't have a life-threatening injury or illness. When I encountered a twig on my path while rollerblading a few years ago, the trip to the urgent care center (with no wait) cost me a little over $100, including X-rays. With the insurance I had at the time, the same care at the ER would have cost me about $1,500.

True, it depends on what's going on, what insurance you have and what services you get. This is why knowing exactly what your health insurance covers and when is very important to your financial situation.

If you have a semi-sketchy insurance plan that is a pain to work with, always inquire about self-pay prices. There are situations in which doctors must charge you a higher deductible or copay if you have insurance, even insurance-lite, than if you don't have insurance at all. Ask to see what the prices are with and without insurance.

Finally, in case you did not know, dental insurance is not part of medical insurance. You need to pay for it separately. A vacation to some appealing foreign country and a new set of teeth is sometimes cheaper than one crown in the US, so that's something else to consider if you need lots of dental work done. Or again, think about getting a spouse with great dental insurance.

Moving on to **car insurance**. If you have a car, you must have insurance. Different states have different minimum requirements for how much you need to carry.

The fact that it is mandatory does not mean that everyone has it. Some states are known for having many uninsured drivers. Hint: Oklahoma and Florida. This is where the term "uninsured motorist" comes into play. Uninsured motorist coverage is for your protection, not the person who is uninsured. If you ever have an accident and it is not your fault but the other person does not have insurance, guess what? Nothing good will happen unless you have uninsured motorist coverage. I strongly advise every one of my clients to carry this coverage, since it could pay off big time one day.

The other two terms to know are *comprehensive* and *collision*. Collision pays when you run into another car or object. Comprehensive covers repairs if your car is stolen, caught in a fire or gored by an angry deer—anything that doesn't involve your car hitting something.

One big thing about insurance that applies to almost every type of coverage is the deductible conversation. What deductible do you choose? You probably noticed that the higher the deductible you are willing to accept, the lower the monthly fee. That makes sense, since the deductible is what you pay before the insurance kicks in. On car insurance, it is typical to see $500 or $1,000 deductibles.

My recommendation is to take the highest deductible you can afford. Could you come up with a $1,000 deductible tomorrow in case of an accident? If the answer is yes, go for it. Here is the kicker: save the difference between the monthly premiums in a secret bank account.

After a few years, you will have a large enough stash to cover your deductible. The main reason I recommend this is because accidents don't happen every day, but you do have to pay your premiums every month. You could be paying for years before you have an accident and need to cover the deductible. By then, what you've saved by accepting a higher deductible might be much larger than the extra $500 you need to pony up out of pocket.

Next, I would like to dedicate some time to the topic of **life insurance**, for two reasons. First, no one likes to talk about death and the need for life insurance. Second, you may have a friend, cousin or uncle who is always trying to sell you some, and I need to give you the breakdown on that.

If you Google "who needs life insurance," you get a million different answers, usually revolving around age and whether or not you have children.

I would like you to think about it from this perspective: if you were to die, is there anyone who would be worse off financially because you were no longer helping with the bills? Many of my students are first-generation college students who pull more than their weight at home. Their parents rely on them to pay the mortgage and keep the lights on. Even though a 21-year-old single college student is not traditionally a target for life insurance, the need in this case is extreme. If something were to happen to the student, the parents might lose their home, as they can't afford the mortgage.

If no one depends on you for anything, then you probably do not need life insurance now.

There are two primary types of life insurance: term life and permanent, which is also known as whole life or universal insurance.

Term life covers you for a specific number of years. You can buy a policy for 20 years, for example. As long as you continue to pay for it every month, if you die within the 20 years, someone (your beneficiary) will get the money you insured yourself for, let's say $200,000. If you are still alive at the end of the 20 years, the insurance company keeps all the money you've paid. If you still need life insurance, you'll then have to buy another policy.

By comparison, a permanent policy is always there until the day when you die, as long as you continue to make payments until it is fully funded (that is, completely paid off). It sounds so much better because you don't "throw money away." It is usually sold this way as well. But personally, I think most people do not need it and usually can't afford it.

Yes, it's going to be there until the end, but the cost is high compared to term. For example, a $300k whole life policy for a 30-year-old can run you about $400 per month, while term life will be about $40 per month. As you can see, there is a huge difference.

I am generally very skeptical of permanent policies for two reasons. Number one, most people who have mortgages and kids usually need quite a lot of coverage. If you try to buy a million-dollar permanent policy, it will be very expensive—to the point that you might not be able to pay your other bills. Thus, many people end up underinsured, with whole life insurance policies that don't cover their needs.

The second reason I am wary of permanent policies is the way they are sold as investment products. I am all for buying life insurance because we need life insurance—not because we need investments. If I need investments, I buy investments. When a high school buddy calls out of the blue, invites you for coffee and then asks you about life insurance, remember what he is after: commissions. A permanent policy pays him much more than a term policy, so guess which one he will try to push on you?

I don't want you to think that permanent life insurance does not have its place. There are situations where it is appropriate. For example, if you get a whole life policy and then develop some disease that makes you uninsurable, then yes, it may pay off. There are also some tax implications that make whole life insurance advantageous for wealthier households. But get a second opinion on what makes the most sense for you—from someone who is not getting paid to sell you on the benefits of the policy.

How do you determine how much insurance to get? Figure out how much your family would need to pay off all debt and to live on until your children finish college or your spouse can support them independently. For example, if your family spends $80,000 per year to live on and your child is seven, you would need to cover about 15 years of expenses. Ignoring inflation, this translates into $1.2 million of coverage. But if money is tight, figure out how much you can afford, build that amount into your monthly cash flow plan and at least get that. Even $200k to $300k would do miracles if you are the sole breadwinner and your mortgage is about that much. At the very least, your family will have a place to live.

If you want to buy insurance, you can do so through work or on your own. I don't recommend work insurance if you are young, healthy and can pass a medical exam because you can usually get cheaper coverage as well as a policy that is locked in for a specific number of years somewhere else. If you go through work and quit your job later, you will lose your cheap insurance. At that point, you will be older, which means you will pay a higher price. I made this mistake once and learned my lesson.

If you happen to be on the receiving end of a policy (you were named as the beneficiary, and the policyholder dies), all you have to do is call the insurance company, provide the death certificate and a copy of your ID and complete a form or two. The insurer will either send you a check or direct deposit the money into your checking account. The proceeds of a life insurance policy are normally not taxable—in other words, you get to keep the entire amount.

Other kinds of insurance deserve to be mentioned. Some to consider are **renter's insurance**, which is cheap but can pay off if something happens to your things while you are a tenant; **short-term and long-term disability** (usually much cheaper when obtained through your employer); and an **umbrella policy**. They are worth looking into, so when you have some extra time, do some research and see if they might be right for you.

Finally, let's talk estate planning. It is probably the last thing you care about, but it really depends on which end of the situation you find yourself on. If I am dead, I doubt I will care if I had a will, but this is not really for me, is it? These documents make sure whoever is left behind can take care of things without endless amounts of hassle. I know that one day, I will be in charge of my parents' estate, so I make sure their stuff is in order to make my life easier.

With that introduction, here are the documents you should consider having if you are over 18:

- A will. This tells the executor (the person you put in charge after you die) what to do with your stuff. What's going to happen to your comic book collection? To your cat? To your old Toyota?

- A durable power of attorney puts someone in charge of making financial decisions if you can't function and make these decisions yourself. Who do you trust with your money?

- An advanced healthcare directive, also known as a living will, does the same concerning medical decisions. If you are in the hospital, who do you want in charge of deciding to pull the plug?

If you go to a lawyer, many will tell you that if you have assets above a specific threshold, you also need a trust so your assets do not go through probate.

Let me translate that: Let's say you own a house that's worth $200k in California, and it's in your name only. If you die, the court will decide what to do with it. (The California probate limit is $150k.)

I am not a lawyer, but my personal take on this is that as long as everything is titled to avoid probate and you have beneficiaries on everything, then you are probably okay without a trust. In my case, since I am married, my husband is the beneficiary of all my accounts, and our houses are titled jointly (that is, are in both our names), his life will not become a financial nightmare if I die. Once there is only one of us left, however, a trust must be put in place, because whoever is left behind does not need the headache of dealing with our three houses.

But, we do have a trust after all, because I am one of those people who likes to be prepared.

My $.02

Are there types of insurance that are not needed? For example, is gap insurance on my new car really a smart financial idea? How about pet insurance?

I am usually skeptical about anything car dealerships try to sell me. I don't think there is a more financially painful experience out there than buying a car from a dealership. That said, you'd be happy to have gap insurance if you total your car soon after you purchased it. As you know, your new car loses value fast once you buy it. If you have a loan on it, you've barely made a dent in that loan after a few months, but your car is worth much less. That's where gap insurance comes in handy. I've personally never bought it because I figured the probability is small of my car being totaled and it being my fault or the other person not having insurance. If you must get it, I recommend calling your insurance company first to see if you can get it there or though the lender rather than at the dealership. The cost will usually be lower.

Pets? Well, it depends on who you ask. My cat has probably been to the vet five times in his nine-year life. But my sister's puppy spent half of his first year there, and her pet insurance saved her a lot of money. If you have a puppy, I hear it is a good thing to have because of the number of shots and checkups in the first year. Pet insurance will probably run you $30 to $50 per month.

Your Bullet Point To-Do List

- Invite yourself over to your parents' house and ask them about their estate plan, the life insurance they have and the beneficiaries on all their accounts, including 401k(s) and IRAs and what would happen if they were to die. There is a good chance you will be involved, so it is important to have this conversation.

- Figure out what type of car insurance you have. Log into your insurance company website and check your coverage and deductibles.

- Look into your medical insurance. What exactly does it cover? How much are your deductibles and copays? Try to figure out what you'd have to pay if you had an accident and ended up in the emergency room.

Chapter 7

The tax excitement

Controlling the things you can

For the longest time, I prepared my tax returns in TurboTax because I liked changing things and seeing how it affected the amount I owed. I wanted to understand how taxes are calculated and what can be done to reduce them. I even read an 800-page book called *How to Pay Zero Taxes*.

This is not a tax preparation chapter; these days, there is no need, as there is plenty of software to do it for you. Instead, I would like to give you a few pointers and opinions about tax-related things.

Let's start with the big question: why is everyone so afraid of taxes and the IRS?

One of the reasons is summed up in a quote I saw on Twitter during tax season: "I'm glad school taught me the Pythagorean theorem instead of how to do my taxes. It's come in really handy this Pythagorean theorem season."

The US has the most complicated tax system in the world. It does not collect that much in taxes, and the IRS is stretched thin, but if you become a tax accountant, I promise you will have a job for years to come. Most people know very little about taxes and are intimidated by the topic. There is no need for that.

Should you do your taxes by yourself or have someone do them for you? If you do have someone do them for you, who do you choose?

If you have a reasonably straightforward situation with W-2 (employment) income and not much else, and if you do not make much money, you can try to find a local VITA clinic. They are associated with universities and will do your taxes for free. They do have an income threshold you need to be under.

Here is where you can find available sites: https://www.irs.gov/individuals/free-tax-return-preparation-for-you-by-volunteers.

Many people, including me, have used TurboTax at one point. But if you have a complicated situation with many extra things (called schedules) like I do, TurboTax is not going to save you much money. My accountant charges me pretty much the same as TurboTax does.

If you want someone to do it for you, look for a CPA (certified public accountant) or an EA (enrolled agent). These are the people most qualified to do tax returns. I am a big fan of EAs because they do nothing but taxes; they can file them for you and can represent you with the IRS if you are audited. Some states (like CA) also have a special certification that allows people to prepare your taxes, but the two mentioned above are universal. You can find a good enrolled agent in your region here: http://taxexperts.naea.org/.

Whoever does your taxes, you want to make sure the person you choose is willing to put his or her name on the return instead of yours. "Self-prepared" on the bottom means that you are responsible for what's on that return, even if someone did it for you and it is incorrect. When you use TurboTax, you are self-preparing and taking responsibility for your return. If you are not sure about what to do, find someone who is good at this and can help you out. If you need a referral, try to get it from someone who knows some tax or financial planning. Don't ask your doctor who has no idea if his accountant is good but thinks "he is a good guy." (Yes, this is a true story a client told me.)

Where You Live Is a Big Factor in What You Pay

The next topic to discuss is the state where you choose to live. What does that have to do with taxes? A lot. Imagine that you graduate from college, get your first paycheck and expect lots of money. And then you see your first direct deposit and how much is coming out in taxes. This is where you start to cry.

Where you live has a lot to do with how much you pay in state tax. Here is a good source to calculate what your pay would be if you were to live in a different state: https://www.adp.com/tools-and-resources/calculators-and-tools/payroll-calculators/salary-paycheck-calculator.aspx.

Anyone who knows me knows my big love for Florida and my big dislike for Los Angeles and California in general. Like anyone else who lives in SoCal, I like living here, but I can do so much more in Jacksonville, FL. There are many online calculators to figure out how much more.
Here is one:
http://money.cnn.com/calculator/pf/cost-of-living/index.html.

Based on the cost of living and the cost of housing, making $100k in Los Angeles is the same as making $71k in Jacksonville. If your salary does not adjust according to your location (and I am yet to see salaries fully adjusted to expensive locations), this means you will be 30% poorer in LA compared to Jacksonville. If you have job flexibility, why would you do that to yourself especially if you do not LOVE the place where you live?

As you are deciding on your next job, in addition to the cost of living (particularly housing prices), consider the state tax (or lack of it) and the sales tax. If you want to own property, also keep property taxes in mind. There is a big difference between property taxes in New York and Alabama.

What You Need to Know about Deductions

The government offers incentives for specific things like buying houses, looking for jobs or saving for retirement. Some of these deductions are available to everyone, whether you itemize (aka spend more time on taxes) or not. They are called "above the line" deductions. Others are only available if you itemize the deductions. Those are called "below the line" deductions.

So, what are the ways you will pay less in taxes? Here is the list of all itemized deductions currently available: https://www.irs.gov/credits-deductions/individuals#itemized.

Each of us decides if they want to take the standard or the itemized deductions. Don't worry, the software you are using will default to the approach that is best for you. There is much more to do if you itemize your deductions (or, in other words, look for specific ways to decrease your taxes).

One of the things no one explained to me when I was young is that there is this whole second tax world in the US called "alternative minimum tax." It is literally an alternative tax code intended to make sure that we do not take too many deductions and end up paying too little tax. If you are making over a specific income threshold and are taking lots of itemized deductions, this could apply to you. TurboTax will calculate both ways, and you must pay the higher amount. Unlike the usual progressive tax system, the AMT system is more or less flat. You will pay either 26% or 28% of your income.

I found this out the hard way the first year I was hit with the AMT tax and all my deductions were no longer worth much. After you do all that work and are ready to file your taxes, the software will say, hold on, let me see if you are paying enough, by doing a completely separate calculation. If it determines you didn't pay enough by filing your taxes the "regular" way, it will make you do it by using this alternative tax system.

There is currently talk about getting rid of this secondary tax system with the new tax proposal, but we will see if any of those changes will actually happen.

My $.02

How do I know how many exemptions to put on the W-4?

You could use an online calculator to estimate what your refund or payment would be in taxes under the current conditions and adjust your W-4 from there.

Here is the IRS calculator: https://apps.irs.gov/app/withholdingcalculator/.

The bigger question is, what do you want to happen when you file your taxes? Do you want money back? Do you want to break even? Do you want to owe taxes? (You don't.)

Is it better to get money back or break even?

Theoretically, you do not want a big tax refund because it means that you are lending the government money for free instead of using it yourself and earning interest. Practically, we like refunds because they come in a nice chunk of cash we can use to pay off debt, contribute to our IRAs or go on vacation.

It is your call. If you can't trust yourself to save the money, it is okay to get that refund.

Ideally, you would break even. You can use online calculators (like the one above) or even hire an accountant to estimate how much to pay in payroll taxes in order to break even.

The IRS called because I owe money. They told me I must pay it right now or I will go to jail.

Have you ever received an email about a rich Nigerian prince who left you an inheritance and all you have to do is provide your bank account and your Social Security number?

As most people know by now, this is a scam. The same applies when someone calls and tells you they are from the IRS and asks for money. They are good. Sometimes you call back and it appears that you called the IRS (you did not). The IRS will never call you. They will always send you a letter if you are audited or there is some problem with your tax return, etc. Next time someone calls and wants some money from you, claiming they are the government, tell them to go away.

Will I get more money back if I get married?

I don't know where this myth came from. You might or might not be better off if you go from single to married. In most cases, if you marry someone who has a comparable income, it is not good for you. If, on the other hand, you make $130k and marry someone who makes $18k, life becomes much better for you, tax-wise anyway.

The marriage penalty or bonus will depend on how the two incomes combine. Don't listen to someone who tells you that you will be better off just because you marry, without considering your particular situation.

Your Bullet Point To-Do List

- Go to the IRS website and spend some time looking at the deductions you could one day be eligible for. Imagine you are making $100k and then try to legally minimize your tax. https://www.irs.gov/credits-deductions/individuals#itemized.

- Download the 1040 form and complete it by hand https://www.irs.gov/pub/irs-pdf/f1040.pdf. There is no better way to learn about tax than to do it yourself.

- Or, if this sounds like crazy talk, find yourself an enrolled agent at and pretend like you have never read this chapter.

Sometimes, you just have to say: "Not my circus, not my monkeys." This might just be one of those times.

Chapter 8

Student loans are not free money

Yes, you do have to pay them back

There is lots of talk these days about student loans. They are easy to get and hard to pay off. I wasn't familiar with the process personally until my Ph.D., when I had to go through it myself. It was a little confusing and I had to go to the financial aid office a few times to get some questions answered, but overall, it was relatively easy to navigate. Next thing you know, I was handed thousands of dollars per semester to pay for my living expenses.

If you are still in college, try to take out as little in student loans as possible. If you can work through your college years or get scholarships to offset the cost of your education, do.

Nevertheless, when you think about it, $7k per year (which is how much Cal State tuition costs in 2017) over four or five years will cost you the same price as a car. It will not set you back that badly (if at all) in life, assuming you can get a job after college and this degree will at one point have something to do with getting better pay.

But if you are only starting college, you also have the option of going to a community college, paying little, and then transferring to a state school to get that degree for under $20k. Why not do that instead?

I don't want to come across as negative because I really do appreciate student loans when they are used to pay for tuition to get a better job. What I am against is using student loans to finance your spring break trips to Cabo. I can see the temptation, but do you really want to pay off those trips for years to come?

I am totally fine with student loans used properly. I am not okay with using those loans to finance a degree in a field with no job prospects from a private liberal arts college of which few people have heard. I am still unconvinced there is anyone out there who came out of a no-name private college with $150k in student loans and an unmarketable degree who was better off in life financially—or happy about their decision. I do not doubt that the experience of going to such a college was worth it on many other levels, but here we're focusing on the financial aspect.

However, if you are already halfway there and there is nothing you can do because you do need to finance and finish your studies, please try to learn as much about student loans as you can. It will make your life a little easier once you graduate and have to start paying them back.

Here is my primer, the five things about student loans that make it clearer what to expect:

1. *You can have federal loans* (for which no one needs to cosign), *and you can have private loans* (for which your parents or spouse will probably have to cosign if you don't have the income and the credit score to qualify). Everyone qualifies for the federal loans; not everyone qualifies for private loans. Federal loans also come with protections and perks, such as various options for repayment. Everyone pays the same interest rate for federal loans, and that rate is set every summer.

   You can find the current rates here: https://studentaid.ed.gov/sa/types/loans/interest-rates.

   By comparison, we all pay different rates for private loans. The better your credit score, the lower the interest you pay.

   There are also PLUS loans your parents can take out to help you pay for college. I am very much against parents taking loans for their kids, and I advise my clients against it. Your parents need to save for their retirement. Too many families sacrifice their retirement by paying too much for their kids' college educations when there are cheaper ways to do that.

2. *Federal loans come in two flavors, subsidized and unsubsidized.* The main difference is who pays the interest while you are a student. If you are lucky enough to get subsidized loans, the government will pay your interest until you graduate. With unsubsidized loans, you are responsible for the interest from the day you receive the loan, which is why you end up owing more money when you graduate than you borrowed.

Obviously, you want the subsidized ones first, if you can get them, because that's like taking an interest-free loan while you are still in school. Whether you qualify for subsidized loans or not is based on the income reported on your tax return or your parents' tax returns in previous years.

In other words, it is based on need and determined after you file your FAFSA every year, by October 1st. (FAFSA is a form that everyone who wants federal financial aid needs to fill out.) https://fafsa.ed.gov/.

Federal loans also have many layers of protection associated with them. For example, if you lose your job, you can defer the payments without penalties for up to three years.

The Consumer Financial Protection Bureau is a great resource to find more about specific information related to student loans and what they are about:

https://www.consumerfinance.gov/ask-cfpb/category-student-loans/.

3. Know what your payment is going to be once you graduate. I am always surprised when I do this exercise with my students and see how far some of their numbers are from reality. For example, if you have federal loans at around 6% and you accumulated $60k, you will need to pay about $666 per month for the next 10 years. That's two car payments, people.

No problem, you tell me, I will stretch it over 20 years, so my payment is lower. That would be $429 per month, and by the time you pay it off, you will have paid $43k in interest in addition to the $60k you borrowed. $103k and 20 years and you are free. That's a house somewhere in Ohio.

To estimate your payment and play with the numbers, use this calculator: https://studentloans.gov/myDirectLoan/repaymentEstimator.action.

4. It's hard to get rid of student loan debt even if you declare bankruptcy. You often hear that it's impossible, but that is not completely accurate. There are ways, but they are long, expensive and hard.

If you plan on bankruptcy, take all the cash available on your credit cards, pay off your student loans and then declare bankruptcy. I am just kidding about this one. Don't take more student loans than needed, please, and if you do, make sure there is a good reason.

Be responsible. Take as little as you can in student loans to get through college, find a cheaper option for schooling and get some help when it's time to pay the loans back. Some people specialize in finding you the best way to pay back your loans. I am not an expert on student loans, but if you need help, let me know, and I will give you a list of people who have been vetted to do this. For about $500 to $1000, you can get a solid analysis done. Trust me; it is worth the cost if it can save you a few thousand dollars or a few years in payments.

5. Think twice about taking on private student loans in addition to the federal ones. The federal government is reasonably generous with the federal ones—so why do you need more? Do a cost/ benefit analysis to see what jobs, salaries and opportunities you will have after getting a degree that requires the extra loans versus the costs and the pain of paying those loans back.

By the way, federal loans are only available to US citizens and permanent residents. If you are an international student, you have to look into the private market.

Paying the Man

Once you graduate, it will be time to pay those loans back. Federal loans have a million options for repayment. Maybe not a million, but close to it. The options available to you depend on when you took the loan out. This is where I advise you again to pay someone to find the best options, especially if money is tight or you are in a field that qualifies you for loan forgiveness.

If you don't know what I am talking about, it is worth a Google search. Teachers, social workers and people in similar professions may have a portion of their loans forgiven after working for a nonprofit for a specified number of years.

If there is no way to have part of your loans forgiven or if an alternative repayment plan does not make sense (or you don't qualify), then you need to deal with the 10-year standard repayment plan. Is it worth it to keep your existing loans or should you refinance? There is also something called consolidation (if you have many smaller loans), but someone still needs to tell me what the point of that is in 2017 with streamlined federal loan administration.

Let's talk consolidation first for 30 seconds. The most important thing to realize is that you will not lower your interest if you consolidate. When you consolidate your loans, you just take the weighted average of all your loans and end up with one payment rather than many smaller ones. Ten years ago, convenience might have been a big selling point. These days, with online payments and easy access, as well as direct payment, it is a non-issue. But if you want to read the federal government's pros and cons and some extra information on consolidation, go here: https://studentaid.ed.gov/sa/repay-loans/consolidation.

By the way, if you still have loans from 10 or 20 years ago, consolidating for the ease of a single monthly payment and logging into one website for information may be worth it. But for anyone who has taken loans in the last few years, this is a non-issue, as mentioned.

Private consolidation, on the other hand, is refinancing, like mortgage refinancing. You effectively pay off the old lender and move your loans to a new lender, aggregating them all into one loan in the process. You cannot be delinquent on your federal loans if you want to make the switch. There are many companies that do this. I went through Common Bond when I decided to refinance my federal loans into a private one about three years ago. (See more on this decision in the *My $.02* section). SoFi, RDB and Earnest are a few of the other big lenders, but new ones are coming onto the market every day.

A question I get all the time is how to pay off student loans faster. But the first question should be if it makes any sense to pay the loans faster at all. This is where some student loan experts come in handy.

With my students, I usually go through this process to help them make the decision about what to do with their loans:

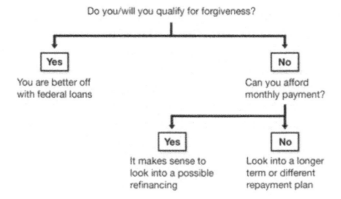

Should you consider refinancing?

Do you/will you qualify for forgiveness?

Yes

You are better off with federal loans

No

Can you afford monthly payment?

Yes

It makes sense to look into a possible refinancing

No

Look into a longer term or different repayment plan

- Do you or will you qualify for any forgiveness? I don't know what will happen in the future, but I am sure my friend who is a social worker has a better chance of qualifying for relief, based on her profession and income, than someone with a degree in computer science and a corporate job.

- If not, figure out what your payment options are if you don't do anything. Can you afford that monthly payment? If not, look at lengthening the term of the loan or refinancing on the private market to get a lower interest rate.

- If yes, ask yourself if it still makes sense to consider the refinancing option. Going from federal to private loans is not for everyone, but it may be worth it under the right circumstances.

- If you know you must pay your loans back no matter what—for example, there is no benefit in paying as little as possible now because you will not qualify for any forgiveness in the future—then consider paying faster. Remember that you must balance this against other goals you might have, such as buying a house, having a baby or vacationing around the world. Or maybe none of these things are as exciting to you as being debt free.

That's it—now just pay them off!

My $.02

My refinancing story

I promised to tell you why I refinanced my student loans, and here is the story. I was lucky enough not to need any loans for my undergrad (thank you Jacksonville University for that full academic scholarship) or for my MBA (thank you to my corporate job).

I did, however, managed to accumulate $64k in student loans during my four years as a Ph.D. student, mostly because when you are a Ph.D. student, you work for the school for $25k per year rather than somewhere else for much more than that.

All my loans were federal and unsubsidized. So, in November 2013, six months after graduation, my first bill from FedLoan Servicing said I had to start paying back $735 per month.

All my loans were at 6.8%, which to me is high-interest debt. But this is what you get when everyone is paying the same interest: the people who pay back their loans subsidize the ones who will not. I was also on the standard, default 10-year repayment plan.

Frankly, I did not do anything at the time except setting my payment on auto-pay, because you get a 0.25% discount on the interest rate if you do, and forgot about it. I budgeted the money into my monthly expenses and moved on in life, knowing that my extra money was going to go to the remodel of the house we just bought instead of extra student loan payments.

Almost two years later, after the remodel was done and private refinancing lenders started popping up everywhere, I decided it was time to tackle my student loans. Oh yeah, I forgot to mention this was also when my husband finished paying off his loans of $106k. It sounds like a lot, but when you are training to become a pilot, at least half of the total is flight costs. It took him eight years, and I am very proud of him for doing it this fast.

In September 2015, I started looking into SoFi and Common Bond, which were the two companies everyone was talking about. When interest rates are dirt low and you are paying 6.8%, you start asking questions—and if you don't, you should. After talking to both companies, I decided to go with Common Bond (the only reason I went with them is that I got a $250 referral bonus, so yeah, good decision-making). The interest rates both companies quoted me were the same.

I decided to go from a 10-year, 6.8% fixed-rate federal loan with eight more years to go in my payment plan to a five-year, 1.99% variable-rate private loan. When I tell this to some people, they are appalled, but hear my thinking.

Here are the facts:

1. The nature of my profession (college professor) means that losing my job is hard to do. If it

happens, I have a long time to find a new one, so I wasn't concerned about a high monthly payment.

2. I was okay with a variable rate because it was so much lower than the fixed rate I was paying. I reasoned that in five years (or by the time I pay it off), it was unlikely to go from 1.99% to anything close to 6.8%.

3. I also knew that I was planning to pay off the loan in three to four years rather than five. To do this, I make extra payments whenever possible, after taking care of investments and retirement savings.

As of right now, I am approaching the end of the second year, and the interest rate is at 2.87%. I have tripled my payment as of this month because we are trying to get rid of this debt as soon as possible in preparation for a future pay cut in our family income.

Refinancing federal loans into private ones is not for everyone, but it does make sense in some situations. If you have lots of high-interest loans, this is something you might want to consider after graduation.

Your Bullet Point To-Do List

- If you or your significant other do not have student loans, you are good. Moving on to the next chapter.

- If you do, list all the loans you have and their interest rates and balances as of right now. Are they subsidized or unsubsidized?

- Next, figure out what your monthly payments will be on the standard 10-year plan. Do you feel comfortable with that? Is it too much? Put together a plan—when and how will you pay them off? And don't forget to have a party after you are done.

- Finally, if you have kids, share your views on student loans with them, for their sake and yours, way before they go to college. Have this conversation with them so they understand what they are getting into before they sign up to take on piles of debt.

Chapter 9

Do I buy? Do I rent? Do I lease?

Um, what's up with all these people leasing cars?

First, let's talk about cars. One of the questions I get all the time is, "Should I lease or buy a car?"

I've heard arguments from both sides, and they both make sense. Before I go into the things to consider when making this decision, you need to decide one other thing. What kind of car makes you happy? Are you the type of person who thinks that a $22k RAV4 is a great car for the next 10 to 12 years? Or are you like one of my students who told me that he only feels fulfilled when he satisfies his need for change and so he always wants to have a new car? Your best choice in leasing versus buying will be determined by what type of person you are.

My take is that if you are going to get a car and keep it forever and that car is going to be a Toyota, then no calculation I am going to produce will ever suggest that you lease it. Buying it is the right decision.

However, if you are going to get a new BMW every three to four years, a leased car will probably make much more sense. The longer you keep the car and the cheaper the price tag, the more the buying decision makes sense. It's that simple. But let's consider some of the details now.

Some of the benefits of leasing are:

- A lease payment is lower than a buy payment on the same car.
- You can get brand new cars every three to four years, as your lease matures.
- There is less headache associated with maintaining the car.

However, when you buy a car, you get to torture it as much as you want and no one is going to charge you extra for those scratches. More importantly, once you pay it off, it is yours to enjoy until it dies—with no monthly payment. That must be worth something, right?

The most I've ever paid for a car in my life was $22,000, and I've now driven it for nine years with an expected two or three more to go, so you can understand why leasing, to me, is crazy talk.

This is not the case for my student, who said he has made peace with the fact that he is choosing to make a car payment indefinitely and that, if his income never improves, he will have to do less of the other things he enjoys, like traveling, shopping for clothes and eating out with friends.

Again, it comes down to what you value and want in life. If it's an impressive car, the lease conversation takes on a completely new tone.

If you do buy a car, one thing to consider is whether you need or want a down payment. I am so against any car down payments that it's a little obsessive. But I just don't understand why anyone would put money down when interest rates are as low as they have been for the last 10 years. If you have a good credit score and don't have to make a down payment, then don't. Just don't. Go and do something better with the money. (I am obviously assuming you can afford the monthly payment without it.) Even better, if you are flexible about the car you want to buy, look for the 0% or something close to it, like 0.9%, financing available on selected models each year. Get that and milk it for as long as you can; no need to prepay your car. Instead, go and invest the money in a high-yield savings account and make 1.3%. It's still better math.

Home Sweet Home

It is time to move on to the homebuying process and all that entails. There are lots of people out there who think that a house will make you rich. However, as much as people invest in houses, the stock market might be a better investment over the long term than a typical house—and in many cases, it requires less time and potential stress on your part. That said, property can increase greatly in value if you buy in the right place and at the right time.

Before we get into the process, therefore, figure out if it makes sense to buy at all. The financial component is relatively straightforward. Compare the rent on a place that you are okay living in to how much house you can afford for a comparable monthly payment. Make sure you incorporate all the costs of owning a house into the calculation, such as property taxes, insurance, maintenance and association fees. The *New York Times* has a very good calculator. Search for "Is It Better to Rent or Buy New York Times calculator," and it will show up on the very top of the search results. Spend some time playing with it even if you are not considering buying a place anytime soon.

Normally, cheaper real estate markets sway your decision toward buying and more expensive markets toward renting. I have a client in New York who is paying $2,300 in rent for a two-bedroom apartment. Buying a place she would like as much would translate into a mortgage of about $3,600—plus the additional expense of owning a home. Is it worth it to pay an extra $1,300 for a comparable space in the same neighborhood? Financially, it is not. But when you are buying a home, there is more than just finances to consider.

Making the Leap

Let's say you've decided to buy a house. First question: how much is your down payment and where is that money coming from? Historically, to qualify for a conventional mortgage, homebuyers couldn't borrow more than 80% of the property's value from any source. In other words, at least 20% of the purchase price had to be their own money, upfront—the down payment. These days, you can get conventional loans with 5% down, FHA loans with 3.5% down and VA loans with 0% down if you are a veteran.

When you put less than 20% down, you need to pay something called private mortgage insurance or PMI. PMI can potentially add a few hundred dollars a month to your mortgage. It is usually about 0.5% to 1% of the loan amount. Once your house appreciates significantly or you pay down the mortgage to below 80% of the value of the house, you can remove your PMI.

In some cases, it does make sense to pay the PMI rather than put the 20% down. The last time we bought a house, the interest rates were so low that it did not make any sense to put more than 5% down on a conventional loan. It's hard to justify putting cash into a 3.75% mortgage rather than in the stock market, where, over the long term, I expect about two times as much in returns. More importantly, we were planning to remodel and knew the home's value would increase significantly in a short period of time, so I could remove the PMI fast. Despite having the cash available, sometimes you put less than 20% down because it makes sense.

No matter how much you put down, you still need to have plenty of cash to buy a home. Saving for a house seems like a huge task, especially if you are starting out. Where do you get the 5%? And don't forget, you also need closing costs. Those will vary by state. For example, let's say you want to buy a house for $180k. If you put down 10%, you need to have $18k for the down payment and another $8k (approximately) for closing costs, a total of $26k to close the deal. This is in Florida, where there are no unusual closing costs. I recently worked with someone in New York whose closing costs were astronomical.

But back to the down payment: where do you get the money from? If you have relatives who are willing to give you some, the gift can be used for a down payment. If not, you need to save, as borrowing for a down payment doesn't work. The banks and regulators want to see that you have some skin in the game. This is where having a budget and sticking to it is very important. You need to figure out what kind of house you can afford, based on the monthly payment as well as the down payment and closing costs.

When it comes to figuring out how much your monthly mortgage costs and down payment will be, you have a few choices. There are many online calculators, but they may not know the exact taxes, insurance and other costs, so you need to adjust the numbers. Otherwise, you will get a number that is not real. I don't trust them for that reason, but if you must use one, go to Redfin, at https://www.redfin.com/, find the house you like and press on custom calculations. Then you can change the numbers to reflect current tax rates and insurance, for example.

The sooner you do the calculations and know what you need, the sooner you can start saving for a home, if that is important to you. Be prepared for it to take you a few years to get there.

If you decide that buying a house is the way to go, you will need a mortgage. As you shop, pay attention to those closing costs—it is not just the interest rates that may differ between lenders. Negotiate anything you can, especially if other lenders are offering better deals.

A good way to start the process is to find a local mortgage broker who can help you choose the best loan for your needs. I usually recommend interviewing two to three brokers to compare prices, fees and costs before committing. Your real estate agent can give you a few names.

Finally, as you start to get excited about that new home, be aware that you will need money for things like new blinds, a new fridge, and a new who knows what. Budget some money so you do not max out your credit cards the month after moving in. Remember that those 2,600 square feet will need to be furnished, and that's not cheap either.

One of the things you will need to decide when getting a loan is how long you want the mortgage term to be. The most common terms are 15 and 30 years. A 15-year mortgage will have a lower interest rate than a 30-year mortgage. Unless you are buying a place where you can comfortably afford the mortgage pretty much no matter what, I recommend taking a 30-year loan and paying it off faster if you really hate debt.

You never know when you might lose your job or have a costly emergency, and having a 15-year mortgage adds extra pressure. Instead, choose the 30-year and then put all the extra money into the principal to be done much faster than you signed up for—if you must. (You may remember from a prior chapter that I am not big into prepaying low-interest mortgages.)

There is a lot to think about when you buy a home. My husband and I move a lot, but we made sure that no matter what, we could rent out the houses we'd bought relatively easily to cover the mortgage. If you buy a home, thinking about where you want to be in three, five and 10 years is a factor you should consider. One of my clients bought in a place that allowed no renters (ever) and had to move for a new job. She paid $215k for the property in 2003 and ended up selling it for $69k in 2009. Timing was bad, the job market was bad and the housing market was disastrous. You can't always outwit bad luck, but consider as many what-if scenarios as you can. You never know what may turn up in a few years.

One last thing I would like to mention is the escrow concept.

"You will need to set up escrow," is what the closing agent told me when my husband and I bought our first house. What is this escrow thing? Nothing to worry about. It is just a separate account from which the mortgage company can pay the taxes and the insurance on your house. Otherwise, once or twice a year, you will have another bill to pay, and many of us are not great about saving money for things like taxes and insurance.

Instead, the mortgage lender will spread the amount over 12 months and add it to your monthly payment. At the end of the year, if you paid too much, they'll send you back a check for the difference. If you paid too little, no worries, your taxes will still get paid, but your monthly payment will go up next year to recoup the shortage. Every December, you will get a statement with an overage (and a check) or a shortage (and a notice of an increase in payment), and every spring, your mortgage payment amount will adjust.

My $.02

What do you think about buying a new car?

I am totally okay with it. There is depreciation in the first year and driving the car off the lot makes it worth much less, but the longer I keep it, the less important this becomes. As I always plan to keep my cars for about 10 years, I am absolutely fine with a brand new car. I want it, so let me have it!

What do you think I should do if I am not a car enthusiast or car status seeker?

You should buy a car and keep it for as long as possible. Also, try to buy the cheapest car that's going to make you happy. Most people say that after a few weeks or months, the enthusiasm of having a new car wears off, but you still have a payment for a few years. Make yourself the happiest you can be, with the least amount of debt.

Can I negotiate the price of the house? The car?

Everything is always negotiable. Depending on the time of year and the type of market, you may have more or less pull in the negotiation process, but it never hurts to try.

So far, my husband and I have bought four houses. We ended up paying under the list price for all four of them, but the discount varied by a lot, from 2% to 11%.

In some cases, if the market is very tight for buyers, you might end up paying even more than the asking price. I would avoid buying a house in such a market, but sometimes you just have no choice.

That is why having a great real estate agent is important. Becoming a real estate agent is not hard, so it is essential to interview a few. I have seen some who were amazing and some who were terrible.

The difference in commission the real estate agent makes if you pay $160k or $170k is negligible, but to you, it is an extra $10k. Find someone who is willing to fight for you and who knows what she's doing. There are plenty of great agents out there—you just need to find one.

Seems like a Federal Housing Administration (FHA) loan is a great deal, with a small down payment. Am I missing something?

Yes, you only have to put down 3.5%, but this comes at a price. You are now stuck with a PMI premium for the life of the loan (until you pay it off, refinance or sell the house). This is huge if you are going to keep the house forever and not refinance it anytime soon. If you are selling the house in three years, not a biggie.

The standards to qualify for FHA loans are a little less stringent than for conventional loans. I usually tell people that this is a loan for those who can't qualify for a conventional loan because if you have a great score and income, you will, in most cases, be better off on the conventional side. But, like almost everything else, there are situations where it makes sense.

For the person who bought a house we sold a few years ago, it made complete sense. Talk to someone who knows about loans and financial planning.

By the way, if you have a bad credit score and are rebuilding it, you can get an FHA loan with a score of at least 580, lower than the conventional threshold.

Your Bullet Point To-Do List

- Go to Redfin or Zillow (or any other similar home search website) and search for the type of house or condo you would like to buy.

- Play with the numbers to reflect the interest rate you would get based on your credit score (check Bankrate.com if you are not sure), the average taxes in that city and the applicable insurance. Finding these numbers may require some Google searches and investigation or a call to a local mortgage broker.

- Figure out how much you need to save each month to get the down payment and closing costs for the purchase. Again, you might have to Google closing costs in the area or talk to a real estate agent to get an idea.

Chapter 10

How to find a financial adviser when you are not rich

Buyer beware

I believe that spending a few hundred dollars and getting help that will save you thousands of dollars is a no-brainer. But if I wasn't in this industry, I guess I probably wouldn't even know what spending a few hundred dollars can do.

For example, you can get a "quick start" (or basic plan) from many advisers for about $500 to $1,000. This is a mini-plan that focuses on a few of the key areas you need help with. I strongly believe that someone who knows what she is doing will get you way more in returns that the money you spend. If nothing else, you should leave more organized and knowledgeable than when you came in. It will not be a full-blown plan, but frankly, not everyone needs a full-blown plan.

This is something to look into if you just need to figure out one or two things. For example, if you do not know how to select investments for your 401(k), please pay someone a few hundred dollars because you will net thousands, if not hundreds of thousands, of dollars over the next 30 to 40 years from this one decision.

This is probably my favorite service that financial planners offer because it makes something confusing accessible to everyone.

Finding the Right Adviser for You

There is so much confusion about this field. Let me give you just a glimpse into my world. I am a financial adviser, so, obviously, I believe in the profession. But I hate the term, since it is not regulated, so anyone can call himself or herself a financial adviser.

I want to try to explain who is who, when to go looking for help, and how to find someone who is good for you.

The first classification of advisers is based on what they do. Some people manage money, some plan your life, some sell products to take care of some need. The terms financial planner and adviser are used interchangeably. Neither one of them means anything. My grandma, who has never read one word of finance, can legally go around telling people she is a financial planner. Or adviser. Or guru. Or life coach.

There are many designations out there, but it is pretty well accepted that a certified financial planner has the minimal level of knowledge necessary to have a conversation about your finances. That designation is maintained and regulated by the CFP Board. The certification requires lots of formal education and passing a six hour exam, as well as ongoing continuing education. If I were looking for an adviser, I would first ask if he or she is a CFP or working towards becoming a CFP.

This is my minimum required standard to pass. Not every CFP is amazing, and not every adviser who is not a CFP is bad. I know plenty of people who are not CFPs and are fantastic, but I would still insist on a CFP because how else would you know if they're qualified? If you don't have the skills to assess someone's expertise, relying on the CFP designation gives you a level playing ground for comparison.

Again, your dentist's recommendation is certainly worth something, but you should vet your planner and interview at least two to three other people before deciding.

Next, we need to talk about who you hire based on what you need. This is like going to a specialist when you see a doctor. If you need money management, look for someone who manages money. If you need a few hours of help with a specific problem, such as buying a house, how to save some money or how to figure out what benefits to sign up for at work, find a financial planner. Many people do both, like a general practitioner. This is fine for most of us in many cases. But there are some situations in which you need someone specialized, like the example on student loans in Chapter 8. In those cases, you should go to a specialist who deals with student loans every day rather than a generalist who does it once in a while.

The second breakdown of financial planners/ advisers/ money gurus is about how they get paid. There is lots of arguing on this topic, and I do not believe any of the ways is best or conflict free, but some are better than others.

There are three broad ways to get compensated: fee-only, fee-based and commission.

- *Fee-only* means you do not sell anything. You get paid by the client: hourly, a set dollar amount that you agree on upfront or a percentage of the money you manage. The big delineator here is that the adviser receives no kickbacks from selling insurance, mutual funds and other things. I am a big fan of fee-only and decided to go this path myself because I simply do not want selling anything to interfere with the advice I give.

  Some people, including plenty of my clients, need to buy insurance. I work with brokers, get a few different quotes and decide which one to go with. People need insurance, and there is nothing wrong with selling it. What I hate is when advisers pretend to do financial planning just to sell something that you might or might not need so they can get a commission for it. It makes the financial planning industry seem like a used car dealership.

- *Fee-based* advisers get their paychecks from commissions and fees directly from the clients. For example, they may get commissions by recommending that you buy insurance or get a percentage of your assets by managing your investments.

- Finally, the *commission* world is transactional. Every time you buy something, the adviser gets a cut. Because of that, there is a strong incentive to sell a lot.

There is no one perfect way to find an adviser, so here are the things to watch for as you look for one:

1. Someone who is fee-only or fee-based and manages money charging something called AUM (assets under management) has an incentive to accumulate as many assets as possible to get a bigger paycheck. I have been in situations where clients had huge 401(k)s at their former employer, for example. Rolling that money under my management would have given me a sizable paycheck, but it didn't always make sense for my client.

2. Someone who sells funds with huge fees (like 5% or 6%) or annuities that are not that great but are sold as if they're hotcakes is evil. At least, that's my take on the situation. There are situations in which annuities (especially fixed annuities) make sense. But it is sad how much time I spend explaining to clients how and when they got screwed by buying an annuity. I

just had a conversation with a client who has an annuity that pays very little; he can't get out of it because after owning it for four years, making about 1% to 2% per year on it, he would lose almost 20% of his investment.

3. Someone who tries to sell you whole life insurance when you do not have the money for it is not to be trusted. I am a big fan of insurance and believe in whole life insurance when the circumstances are right. But I see very few permanent policies that were sold because they were needed and many that were sold because someone needed to get paid.

Once you buy a permanent policy, if you stop paying in the first few years because you realize you can't afford the $400 monthly payment, you are pretty much screwed—you've lost lots of money. If you decide one of these policies is right for you, make sure you will always be able to afford the monthly premium and are planning to keep the policy for a long time.

The Bad and the Ugly

When I was putting the outline of this book together, I got lots of requests to include some information about how to avoid financial scams. Here are some things to look for:

- Be wary of anyone who promises you great (big) or specific returns on your investments. Unless you are buying a fixed annuity, giving specifics is impossible. Who in the world knows what the stock market will return next year? If I knew, I would be a billionaire by now. This is not why you hire a financial planner. Anyone who promises 8% every year, year after year, is delusional, a scammer or both.

- Find someone you like. The best financial planning revolves around a long-term relationship. As mentioned, my minimum requirement is a fee-only (or maybe even a fee-based) CFP or CFP-in-the-making with a few years of experience. Once that requirement is fulfilled, the knowledge will be there to get whatever help you need, so find someone you like to spend time with. I personally dislike salesy-type people who seem more concerned about their appearance and smooth talking than about financial planning. I want my financial planner to be a nerd who reads financial planning magazines for fun, not someone who drives a BMW, wears a suit and projects that lifestyle onto me.

Figure out what you want from a planner and find one to match your preferences. There is someone out there for everyone.

- Interview two to five people. Just as with a doctor, you want someone you trust. Keep looking until you are happy. After all, you are paying them.

- Ask a few questions to help figure out if they'll be able to help you. This is hard to do if you don't have any financial knowledge, but at least ask their beliefs on one money topic and see how well they match yours. Ask what they'll do to make your life better and how they will do it. It is their job to articulate why you should hire them.

- Avoid anyone who tries to make money seem complicated. Your adviser should be able to explain things in a way you can understand—an adviser's job is to make complicated things easy. Don't hire someone who makes things sound fancy.

- Be wary of anyone who promises you anything for free. My biggest warning sign is if someone promises to do financial planning for free—how will that person be paid for all the time he spends on the plan?

It takes about 10 to 20 hours to do a comprehensive financial plan, so unless I am getting paid in some other way, free is not a feasible business model. These people are being paid in some way, so you need to figure out how and where. Nothing wrong with that, as long as you know.

Financial planning has its limitations, just like everything else in life. Striving for balance is important. Financial planners focus a lot on saving money, but the truth is that you need to live and enjoy your life and feel good about your money decisions. As you look for a financial planner, try to find someone whose ideas resonate with yours. If your dream is to sell all your possessions and buy a tiny house, I promise there is a financial planner out there who has done it or hopes to. Try to find that person, and you will find more than just a financial planner—you will find someone who cares about you on a deeper level.

My $.02

But I am not rich yet. Why do I need someone to help me out?

Before I got into this business, I thought that financial planning was for rich people too. Professionally, it was the most wrong I have probably been in my life.

Financial planning is for people who want to make their life a little better. It does not matter where you are: in debt, with a little bit of cash, with a new job, or with lots of money. Financial planning is not only about money management. It is about improving your life just a little bit, day by day and year by year.

What is a reasonable amount to pay for these services?

I get this question a lot. Here is what I think is reasonable. More than anything, it is not just about the price but what you get for that price.

- Hourly planning ranges in price, but I consider $100 to $300 per hour to be acceptable; $300 is high unless you are looking for very specific knowledge not many advisers have.

- Small/focused/quick-start plan. This is a limited plan that focuses on a few issues. I usually like this better than hourly, because you don't have to worry that you will be billed for more hours than necessary. You'll usually see prices ranging from $500 to $1,000 for this service.

- Comprehensive financial planning; a full plan. Again, there is quite a price range, but $1,000 to $3,000 is standard. This usually comes with one year of follow-up. If you are paying $2,000 to $3,000, you should get more than just "here is your plan, buh-bye." The planner should be there making sure you are doing what you are supposed to be doing.

- Plain vanilla money management ranges from 0.7% to 1.5%. There are people who charge more, and I have seen people do it for even less. Anything over 1.25% is a lot. What matters most is what you are getting for the amount you pay. To me, it means full access to whatever you need and not just "give me your money and see you next year." Paying 1% just to park your money somewhere is too much. Getting someone to answer your non-money-management-related questions for 1% is a great deal. Compare what you are paying to what you are getting, and don't forget to look at the cost of the funds you are investing in. I can usually make a very compelling case for someone to move their money from a "big box" firm because I can provide more value for a slightly lower or the same price they charge.

How do I find a money manager who will work with me when I don't have the money to manage?

It is hard to make money on money management until a client has around $200k. Many advisers won't take you on unless you have the assets because they can't break even otherwise.

There are a few good sources to look for advisers who will work with anyone regardless of their assets. Here are those I consider the best:

- The XY Planning Network. Full disclosure: I am part of it. It caters to the younger generation who may not have the assets and want help. Advisers will work with you virtually, and you can find someone who appeals to you. Most advisers offer hourly planning, limited engagement or full financial plans. They are all fiduciaries* and do not sell anything. To be listed, you must be a CFP®. If you are not 70 and do not have a few million dollars, I would start here. If you are reading this book, in other words, you should start here.

  http://www.xyplanningnetwork.com/consumer/find-advisor/

  *Again, jargon alert: a fiduciary is someone required by law to put your interests ahead of her own or his own. Surprise! Not all people who give you financial advice are required to do what's best for you.

- The Garrett Planning Network. I am not part of this network and am not very familiar with it, but its advisers do hourly work and are trusted.

https://www.garrettplanningnetwork.com/

- NAPFA (I am a member). This is a network of fee-only advisers, so again, they can't sell anything. Everyone who is on the XYPN is also going to be here, but not the other way around.

  https://www.napfa.org/find-an-advisor

- The CFP Board. If you have your CFP® certification, you can be listed here. It does not look at the way the people are compensated or the minimum requirements to become a client, so you might need to do some additional vetting.

  http://www.letsmakeaplan.org/choose-a-cfp-professional/find-a-cfp-professional

Your Bullet Point To-Do List

- Go to the XYPN website and find yourself an adviser, even if it is imaginary for now. Once you have a job and need help choosing benefits and your 401(k), come back and hire the adviser you found.

- One more time, find yourself a planner-adviser for the long term.

That's all I got on your to-do list.

PART III:
THE TOUCHY-FEELY
STUFF

Chapter 11

The relationship between money and happiness

It's really all in your head

I have no doubt that financial security is important to a stable life.

You all know the "Money can't buy happiness" quote. Here is a better quote:

"Money can't buy you happiness but it can make you awfully comfortable while you are being miserable."
—Clare Boothe Luce

I agree that money will not make you happy, but a lack of money will surely create stress. If your money house is in order, you might not be happy, but you will be less stressed. Of course, some of us care more about nice things, while others care more about happiness. But at the end of the day, no one wants to be poor.

When I first mentioned to someone that I wanted to include a chapter on the relationship between money and happiness, he was skeptical. After all, this is the realm of philosophy. It kind of goes against the neatness of numbers, math and finance.

I am aware of the issues. But I also know that it is essential to figure out exactly what you want from life and the future—and how money fits into that plan—before any kind of financial roadmap is put in place.

This chapter has fewer "rules to live by" and too many "it depends on you." But this is life. It is not as neat as my financial calculator pretends it is, so let's start and think about a few things that relate to money and happiness.

When I first talked to John, I thought he was the best saver I'd ever met. He saves 30% of his income every month, tries to buy used things when possible and adopted a minimalist lifestyle after watching the documentary *Minimalism*. But after a few more conversations, I also found out that he has a collection of wine he enjoys. For some of the bottles he owns, he paid amounts that many would consider extremely high.

John is a perfect example of why I decided to include this chapter in the book.

Some people prefer to work less even if it comes with making less money. Others prefer to work more and make more money. We might or might not be equally happy, but what is important is that we sat down and thought about what we wanted.

We must figure out how much money we need to make to be satisfied and how many hours of work we are willing to put in to accomplish it. Our results will be very different—and this is exactly why I insist that you calculate your number.

What is the income you need to make yourself happy?

Most of us go through life chasing daily obligations: paying off our car loan, paying off the new Home Depot credit card, saving for retirement, going on vacation, etc., etc. But too few of us consciously assess our spending habits and how those habits relate to our happiness.

Sometimes we encounter a shock-like event that makes us reevaluate and reprioritize our lives and the financial trade-offs that come with it. I encourage you to do it now. Please don't wait for the big event that's going to change your life. Today, start questioning how you spend your time and money and whether your spending habits align with what you perceive to be your happiness.

Here is an exercise you can do as a first step:

- Start by writing down all your ongoing monthly expenses (such as rent, car loan, student loans). I know there are a lot of tools out there for budgeting, and that's great, but do it on paper, since I want you to work through these things later. Trust me; it's easier to do this in an old-fashioned notebook or that Excel sheet I included in chapter 1.

- Now, assign a number from zero to 10, rating how happy this spending makes you. Zero is a complete waste of happiness, and at 10 you are so happy to spend money on this, you can't contain yourself. For example, my current mortgage would be a five for me. It makes me reasonably happy, I have a nice roof over my head, but I am also sure I can live in a somewhat cheaper place and be as happy as I am now, so—five.

  Go through all your boring expenses and grade them. This is a very personal exercise; no one can tell you what makes you happy. I imagine a zero to me would be an expensive gym membership I never use because it's too far away (totally sucks) and a 10 would be $500 I spent for some beautiful professional family pictures. (This is the best money I ever spent.) You get the point. No one knows what makes you happy but you.

- After you are done with all the bills, start writing down your other spending. Go back about three months if you can. If even three months sounds like torture, start with today. Write down everything you buy, every day. Same exercise, same idea. For example, it is 10:40 AM now, and I managed to spend $4.25 on a latte so far. How happy does that make me? An eight. I made my peace with Starbucks a long time ago, and I am okay with paying for lattes. Don't you judge me—this is my happy place.

Just start a note on your phone and record every purchase as you go through the day. You do not need to make any changes yet. Just write it down for as long as you can. Even a day is better than nothing.

Some things will change from day to day. For example, if you are hungry, don't have any food at home and you go to Chipotle and spend $9, it could be rated a 10 because it saved you time and made you happy. The same purchase might be a four tomorrow if you have food at home, are not even hungry and somehow end up at Chipotle again. Go through the exercise every day and assess all your spending, line by line.

At the end of the day, week, or month, look at the things that brought you the least happiness. You decide on the cut-off point. Is it a five? A seven? Something else? Then, start at the bottom, with the zero to three categories, and try to cut out those expenses one at a time. Next month, move to the fours, and so on, until you get to a place where you are satisfied with how you are spending your money MOST of the time.

Here is what will happen if you do this for about six to 12 months: You will have more money. I promise you. You might have more savings, you might start paying off your debt faster, or you might get rid of your debt altogether. You might realize that the high payment on your car is not worth it to you, sell the car and buy a Yaris with a payment of $200. Or you might get a puppy because you finally have money and time for a dog. Who knows what will happen. The world is your oyster.

You will also start questioning every purchase you make. Is that $12 you just spent for a happiness level of three necessary? Of course not. And you will most likely get rid of it soon, but you won't change your habits until you realize what's going on in your life RIGHT NOW.

You might start aligning what you want in life with what makes you happy. If working too much is a problem because you feel like all you do is work to pay bills, you may end up cutting a few expenses and spending more time with your family. Whatever it is, you will end up more satisfied with the way you spend your time in the long run.

Plenty of research shows that time spent on people and activities you like leads to happiness. So maybe we should work on that rather than putting an extra three hours a week into our jobs just to pay for something we don't even care about?

Realistically, this is much easier if you do not have a partner you share bills and a bank account with. People have different priorities, and they usually don't agree with each other. However, you can start on what you control—your own spending and savings habits—until you get to a place where you are ready to bring your partner into the conversation.

For now, focus on your reflections about what's important in your life. The great thing about this exercise is that it doesn't matter how much money you make. It can be applied to any salary and spending level.

One other thing you need to realize is that even if you come up with a perfect financial plan, things will not go 100% the way you want them to. Not everything can be controlled. Life happens. You will deviate from the plan, and that's okay. Adjust when needed.

Think about when it is important to you to be cheap and when it is important to be generous. If you want to donate money to causes that matter, it is okay to do that even if you are cheap in every other aspect of your life. The spending will differ, but the idea is the same. We need to feel like what we do with our money matters. Let's put some thought into it.

Be prepared—your life will not change overnight, but it will change. It will take months. In about six months, you should feel a level of satisfaction and control with your finances and life in general that you do not have now.

The 2015 American Psychological Association poll concludes that "Money continues to the leading source of stress in Americans' life."

Maybe it's time we do something about it?

My $.02

I am 25 years old, two years out of college and I think I want to change my profession. Is it too late now?

Nah, it's never too late. I am 35 and on my third career. Someone I like and admire finished his Ph.D. in his early 60s. Twenty-five is nothing. You can always change what you do.

Think about a financially feasible way to do it. If there is no one to sponsor your lifestyle while you make the transition, maybe continue that boring accounting job while you go to school at night, preferably at the community college or cheap state school. Gradually make the switch.

A switch with a plan is better than a switch without a plan. Your bank account and your future self will thank you.

When do I have to stick to my saving and spending plan and when is it okay to splurge on an emotional buy?

It is a bad idea to spend money you do not have. The instant gratification is normally not worth the stress associated with being in debt and not being able to dig yourself out of the hole. But there is nothing wrong with splurging on something occasionally if it is not going to affect your life negatively. This is just like being on a diet. Two weeks of great eating will not be negated by a piece of cake if you do not use it as an excuse to give up the healthy eating plan. Similarly, after a month of adhering to your money plan, it won't kill you if you end up going out to brunch with your friends or buying a new pair of shoes. If you think about the pleasure derived from the purchase and decide it is worth it, it is okay to go for it occasionally.

Just make sure your long-term plan for financial stability won't be derailed by a short-term decision.

Your Bullet Point To-Do List

- Look at everything you spent money on this week and grade each of the purchases.

- Decide which expenses you do not want to incur again.

- Do the same exercise again and again until you are happy with most of what you spend money on.

Chapter 12

Marriage & money: How to talk finances to each other

---

*"Your money problems would be much easier
to solve if you didn't have another person
to help you solve them."*

I made that quote up, but I am sure the research on money, happiness and relationships supports my conclusion.

Here is what I do know:

- Arguments about money may be the top predictor of divorce (at least, this is what a 2012 study of 4,500 women found);
- Working with clients who are in relationships is more challenging than working with a single person (everyone is convinced their way is the right way); and
- A lot of the issues I have observed so far in dealing with people's finances revolve around their relationship with money and each other and not around what I see as the clear solution to an actual financial problem.

One of my clients told me this story: Her friends are about to get divorced, and they own a house on which they can't agree. They could sell it, get an ample amount of cash for it, split the money and start a new life—or keep the house for a few years until the kids are out of college and can decide for themselves if they want the house.

There is no way I can make a case for keeping the house knowing the financial details of the situation, and yet they are still arguing about it, unable to reach a compromise. This is life when there is another person to consider.

How do you navigate a world in which you have another human being to be accountable to financially?

For the people who are not in that stage of their lives yet, I would also like to talk about how to continue sticking to your plan and working toward your goals when your mom or best friend insists you go out to brunch, on a cruise or shopping. How do you develop or maintain relationships with other people when you are not on the same page financially, without feeling like you are missing out on life? How do you have these conversations or even approach these topics? Do you walk away and find people who have the same money mentality as you?

Let's say you just met someone you are smitten with. You think this is your soulmate, future partner and the best person alive. You seem to like the same music and food, and you want to travel the world together.

Then, two months in, in some random comment, you find out that this person has about $12k in credit card debt, has a 580 credit score and, at the age of 32, has no idea what a 401(k) is.

You, on the other hand, are proud of your 800 credit score and are stashing away about 15% of your income for retirement.

Call me materialistic and boring, but this relationship is probably not going to work out unless one of you changes, and it's not you who needs to change. After your initial infatuation subsides and you start thinking about the implications of that 580 credit score on your future ability to qualify for a mortgage—on the quality of a future life together—a little bit of love might disappear.

But how do you have this conversation? Do you approach it over dinner or wait for some random event? When I was 25, I would probably have said, "No way, I am not going to ask about someone's credit score on the first date."

Now I do not know. And I know it's easier for me because I am in this world all day, every day and I talk about money a lot. But if I were you, knowing all the research on this topic, I would approach the topic sooner rather than later. Even though it's awkward. If you are super-responsible and the other person is not—and more importantly, is not fully committed to positive change—there will be issues down the road, and those issues will need to be solved.

Word of caution: don't dismiss people without knowing their story. There are always exceptions (think of a bankruptcy related to huge medical bills).

You are the only one who knows what you find acceptable and unacceptable. If you both think maxing out your credit cards and declaring bankruptcy is just fine, then we don't have a problem. (Well, we have a huge problem, but that's not the point of this chapter).

Today, I want you to think about what is important in relationships so that you can avoid money arguments and not end up divorced because of those arguments. **I am convinced that the answer to all money fights is the concept of "being on the same page about money."**

It doesn't matter how much money you have or don't have. I work with clients who make $300k and constantly argue about money and with those who make $70k and seem to agree on pretty much everything; it is what you want to do with the money you have that matters.

There are a few discussions that need to happen between partners again and again. Assumptions about how you two want to spend your money don't work; you need to articulate your desires. This is not a one-time conversation. As you get older and your jobs, financial situation, personalities and aspirations change, you need to continue to discuss where you stand. You need to be clear about what is important to you and to consistently align the way you spend your money with your vision for your life.

About a year ago, I got a call from a potential client who wanted to hire me to arbitrate between him and his wife. The idea of talking about money overwhelmed him, so a few years earlier, he put her in charge of all the bills. Except that somehow there was no money to pay all the bills, and yet he still could not make himself participate in money conversations.

Finally, she pretty much told him she was ready for a divorce because it was unfair to her. Google suggested they call me. Listening to their story, I was perplexed. There was certainly not a shortage of income (they were making plenty of money), and there was certainly not a lack of willingness to be responsible (they didn't have extravagant lifestyles). Yet somehow, they were not on the same page about money, and it was affecting their marriage and their happiness.

They are not the only ones. I see it all the time. The easiest part of my financial planning role is running calculations; I have no problems allocating a 401(k) or telling someone if it makes more sense to buy or lease a car. The hardest thing I encounter is dealing with my clients' feelings about money and supporting them. That is why getting on the same page is crucial to your relationship.

This whole conversation so far sounds depressing. By now, you might be thinking: "Inga, we are already arguing about money all the time, please tell me something I don't know."

Here are some things you can start with that will help. You need to have the (#1) "life" and (#2) "things" conversations.

Do you fundamentally agree on what is important in your life?

Do not even mention money at this point.

Do you see yourself happily gardening in the suburbs, taking on contracts as an adjunct professor while your husband works toward becoming the next university president? Does your husband see YOU as the next provost (obviously while he is the president), or building a business empire to be envied by every naysayer in your former job?

I am not going to say that you won't be happy and your relationship won't work out if you are not on the same page, but it won't be easy. A lack of similar ambitions (and the paychecks that go with those ambitions) usually signifies a disconnect in what you want from life.

Assuming you have similar ideas about what is important in life, like you both want to be workaholics, you both want to travel in the summers and work as little as possible, you both want to spend time with kids, etc., let's move to the money part.

Are you on the same page about which material things will bring you happiness?

You can buy happiness—you just need to figure out if it is the same for both of you.

It is very challenging when one person wants a BMW and the other is happy with a Corolla. It's not about the car. It is about the car payment that comes with it and the unfulfilled emotional needs that go with that car payment; it is about what that money signifies to each of you. When there is a big difference in willingness to spend on the same things, no one wins, and everyone is miserable.

The BMW seeker thinks the other person is obsessed with money and can't enjoy nice things in life, while the Corolla person thinks the significant other is taking on unnecessary, perhaps even frivolous, expenses that will derail their plans to retire, work less and enjoy life more.

So who is right? A question I hear a lot is, "Can we afford it?" In most cases, yes, you can afford it—but should you? That's not for me to decide. I don't know what makes you happy, and if I give you my opinion, I will be taking the side of the person who is most like me.

The two of you need to have these conversations and decide what you both want from life. What I can promise you is that making both people happy will be hard, and in the end, neither one of you may feel like you got what you wanted.

Nevertheless, you need to try, because if the person who doesn't want the expensive car feels like money is being wasted, or the person who wants that car feels like their happiness isn't as important to their partner as piling up savings, the relationship will suffer. You may end up with the nicer car or more savings along with, as Dew, J., Britt, S., and Huston, S. (2012) predict, an expensive divorce.

Another question I get all the time is, "Should we join our finances when we get married or not?"

Sorry, people, but it depends. If you've decided to combine your finances, I promise we can find a way to make it work. The big rule is that you cannot question each other's spending habits. This is only possible if there are rules in place; otherwise, I promise you will get resentful. Imagine you are a saver and your new spouse is not. You decide you can live with this, but now you end up saving 30% of your paycheck and she is not saving anything.

It might work for a while, but eventually, especially when you have kids, you will start asking why life is unfair and why she can spend money on things you don't care about while you have to spend yours on school supplies.

How do you solve this problem? Decide on a number that each of you can spend as you wish. The other person has no say and no right to question this spending. If you both get $500 per month on whatever you want, you can never, and I mean NEVER, make fun of your husband for buying video games for $500, and he cannot express disbelief that your hair costs $200 to color.

I've worked with plenty of people who do it together and plenty who keep it separate. It works either way, as long as you have a plan in place.

My husband and I kept our finances separate for the first three years of our marriage, even after we bought our first house together. Eventually, we merged them. Initially, I thought that it would limit my ability to do things, but it does not. It took me a while to get over my hang-ups and the idea that I would lose some control. For a type A person, the control part is a big deal, and it needs to be addressed.

Let's move on to the second part of this chapter and discuss the money conversation you should have with your parents. Ideally, money would have been freely discussed in your house since you were a young child. In reality, many families assume that the kids will pick up these critical skills on their own. I see these kids in my class every day. Very few develop financial skills without assistance. So, if you have or will ever have children, please do them a favor and discuss the topic of money. Teach them about budgets and debt and how to build a good life for themselves.

How about your parents? How often have you had the conversation about your parents' financial situation? You need to have at least one talk, if for no other reason than you might end up being the one in charge of their estate one day. If so, they can make your life easy or miserable by being prepared or unprepared. No one wants to talk about death and money, but you owe it to yourself to bring up this topic.

Occasionally, I'm asked if it's okay to borrow money from your parents. This one is up to you and your parents. If your parents have the means and you can make it a mutually beneficial relationship, why not? One thing to keep in mind is what would happen if you can't pay the debt. Or, if you're considering a loan to someone in your family, if that person can't pay you back. Your relationship will probably suffer. If you do end up lending money to family members, be prepared never to get it back. If you do, it will be an extra surprise.

And how about the friends situation? Let's say we are in a group of friends who hang out all the time and it is normal to go out on the weekend and spend $100 on dinner and drinks. Unfortunately, you do not have $100 and end up putting it on your credit card, wondering how to pay it off at the end of the month and why you can't seem to get ahead in life.

I suggest you do two things:

- First, decide how much hanging out in this particular way means to you. If the pleasure you derive comes from the things you do when you go out, then I suggest you find a way to budget for this money and cut something else from your life.

- If it is the people and not the going out to dinner part you care about, however, then talk to your friends. Explain to them that you can't afford the weekly outings. See if, as a group, you can come up with alternative activities. Maybe one weekend you will go hiking (I hear that's free and healthy), the next week you hang out at someone's house (alcohol is much cheaper at Costco than at a bar), and the third week, you go out for one of your fancy dinners.

And if your friends are not willing to make any changes—then are they really your friends?

I will leave it at that.

My $.02

How do we incorporate kids into the mix and budget and save for them?

Before having kids, I often heard that children are expensive. Now that I have one, I do have an opinion, and I believe you can make it as expensive or as cheap as you want it to be. The one big expense is daycare. If you need childcare, yes, it will be expensive.

However, the actual price of buying things for the baby is not that bad. It depends on what you buy, from where and how much. My kid is just fine with three bottles, five toys and six outfits. I am joking; he probably has 10 outfits. I do not need a $300 device to entertain him—he seems to be just as happy in the pile of laundry.

That's my personal bias, though. If you choose to, you can make a baby very expensive.

One thing you should consider is your child's future. Do you intend to pay for college? In that case, early planning makes sense since it will be cheaper for you in the long run. Please refer to Chapter 5 for options.

I do hear that older children cost more. My client-friend who has a teenager tells me it is no longer about clothes and toys. Things start shifting toward more extracurricular activities, which can get very expensive. For example, her daughter plays volleyball. Getting good enough to play on the high school team (and potentially college) requires tournaments, clubs and lots of expenses. Just one four-day tournament costs about $2k.

Considering the costs of the kind of lifestyle you would like to provide for your children may be a factor in deciding how many you want to have.

Your Bullet Point To-Do List

- If you are in a relationship, talk about what you both think about your levels of satisfaction with your life together and how you spend money. Are there any changes you or your partner would like to see?

- If you have never discussed your parents' financial situation and you know you might be in charge of their affairs later in life, bring this topic up the next time you see them.

- Finally, think about all your friends and if there are any you feel are derailing your financial goals. Have a conversation with them and see if you can make some changes in your future spending habits.

Conclusion

After reading the book, I hope you have a better idea about money, financial planning and how to live a better life.

We all come from different backgrounds and families. Maybe you were raised in a family with good money habits. Maybe you were not so lucky. Regardless of your past, this is the moment that matters. Whatever happened before this point is irrelevant. Start now and make it better from here, whatever *better* might mean to you.

You may find that doing the right thing financially feels good. And because of that, you might start making better financial decisions in the future. Developing your core values, deciding what's important to you and living your life to match those values will make you happier over the long term.

What are the habits we can develop to avoid the costliest financial mistakes?

My fellow financial planner Stefan says: "Stay healthy, exercise, eat well (most people spend most of their money on food/eating out/drinking); strengthen your core values and develop a sense of purpose."

I couldn't agree more. It is easier to create a good life when your life is simple. As you get older and things get complicated, so do the financial aspects of life. Putting a good plan together when you are young will benefit you and the people around you for the rest of your life.

Figuring out money is hard but even by reading this book, you have already decided to do your best to improve your financial situation. If this book helped you in any way, please tell your friends about it. You are now the expert who can make their lives easier.

Thank you for reading. Please feel free to connect with me on social media—I hope to hear from you.

Facebook:
Inga Chira https://www.facebook.com/inga.chira
Attainable Wealth
https://www.facebook.com/AttainableWealth/
LinkedIn:
Inga Chira www.linkedin.com/in/inga-chira

Finally, please consider leaving a review on Amazon if this book was useful to you in any way. I hope to improve the book in the future, and your feedback would be much appreciated.
—Inga.

Disclosure

This book and its content are for personal use only and are protected by applicable copyright, patent and trademark laws. The information provided in this book is for general information only. It is not intended to be used as personal investment, tax or legal advice or recommendations.

All opinions and information included in this book are based solely on sources believed to be reliable. However, you are responsible to verify any information for accuracy, completeness, correctness, timeliness or appropriateness.

You are solely responsible for your own investment and financial decisions, and each investor is responsible for evaluating any information used or relied upon in making his or her investment decisions.

Before making any investment decisions, you should investigate the investments being considered and consult with a qualified investment adviser about your specific situation. The information presented in this book is not to be used as a substitute for professional financial advice.

Investing in the stock market has risks that need to be evaluated for your specific needs. Different types of investments have different types of risks, and it is your responsibility to evaluate the suitability of specific investments and risks to your own financial situation.

The reference to any third party or third-party products should not be construed as approval or endorsement by the author. Although the author has personal preferences, those choices need to be understood and evaluated for appropriateness for your own financial situation.